P9-AQV-508

DO NOT CIRCULATE

Eckhart Public Library

603 S. Jackson Street   Auburn, IN 46706
Phone: 219-925-2414

Patron is responsible for all
material borrowed.

FORT WAYNE'S

FAMILY ALBUM

Bessie Keeran Roberts

CUMMINS PRINTING COMPANY

FORT WAYNE, INDIANA

PUBLISHED 1960

The spirit within communing with past ages has told me these things.

TECUMSEH

A true picture of our times is a permanent contribution to literature and life.

THEODORE DREISER

A gentleman of the right sort will stand hardships better than anybody else.

PARKMAN

CONTENTS

FORT WAYNE'S FAMILY ALBUM

I.
We Follow a Trail

WHEN IN THE early spring of 1833, Hugh McCulloch of Kennebunk, Maine, left his New England home to make his start in the West, there was only one railroad in the New England states. His westward journey, was made by rail from Boston to Providence, thence by steamboat to New York, which he observed was "fast becoming the great commercial city of the Union." The rest of the trip was by steamboat, rail, stage, and finally by packet down the Ohio to Cincinnati, then the river gateway to the West.

What his destination was, which state he would choose for his stopping-place, were as yet undecided. It was the season when the frozen ground was yielding to the touch of the sun, and settlers were heading their wagons and ox-teams toward the western trails. He could only set his course by the great star that burned brightly in the western sky, and give way to the urge that moved restless youth like the rise of sap in the maples.

There were voices calling to high adventure, far places, golden opportunities; there was the trumpet call to duty. There were political philosophies in the air. When the voice of Daniel Webster rolled from the Senate chamber on January 27, 1830, the words, "Liberty and Union, now and forever, one and inseparable," were to become the political religion not only of Abraham Lincoln, but of generations yet unborn.

"Mr. Webster's speech was not merely the great speech of the day; it was a speech that had never been equalled before. It has never been equalled since, in this country or any other," Mr. McCulloch wrote after many years, in his "Men and Measures of Half a Century."

A personal letter written by Mr. Webster in Boston on May 14, 1833, was received and carried by young McCulloch into the new regions he was to see.

"Hugh McCulloch Esq. Dear Sir: Mr. Peabody has suggested that a general letter from me, such as might be written to any

Hon. Hugh McCulloch

friend in the Western states, might be useful to you, in regard to the object of your visit to that part of the country — I have great pleasure in complying with the suggestions; altho this letter may be addressed to you, it is intended to express to any to whom it may be shown, my good opinion of your character, talents and acquirements; and my confident expectation though you settle in that region that you will make yourself distinguished in the community and in your profession.

With friendly good wishes, I am your ob. svt.,

Daniel Webster"

Hugh McCulloch, twenty-four — just two months and two days older than Lincoln — had attended Bowdoin College and practiced law in Boston.

In Cincinnati he met E. M. Huntington, later a United States Circuit Judge, who thought highly of the prospects of Indiana, and influenced him to go on to Madison on the Ohio River. There he showed the letter from Webster to Jeremiah Sullivan, a leading lawyer of the state, "a highly talented Virginian."

There were only two bridges in Indiana, a capitol city with "mud knee-deep in the principal streets where only a few stumps had been removed," and a wilderness road leading north straight through the forest. Toward a destination still uncertain, he set out with new-bought horse, saddle and bridle, after exchanging his trunk for saddlebags. It was when he started out on the Michigan Road, that had been built from Indianapolis to Lake Michigan out of the sale of Miami Indian lands, that he became completely satisfied with the course he had taken.

"Upon entering it (the Michigan Road) that afternoon, I perceived that nothing had been done to make it a road except to open a way through the forest. It was perfectly straight, and the noble trees — nearly a hundred feet in height — stood on either side of it like a protecting wall. The birds were singing blithely, and although my horse was my only companion, the wildness and novelty of the scene acted like a tonic. Long, long years have intervened; a long and busy life is nearly ended, and yet the exhiliration which I experienced as I rode through that magnificent forest, comes back to me as freshly as if it were but yesterday."

For Hugh McCulloch had decided that this was the state

where he would remain. No state, he reflected later, has been more prolific of superior men than Indiana. Especially did he respect the circuit-riding lawyers of Indiana and Illinois. There was Oliver P. Morton, the great war governor of the West, and the circuit-riding lawyers such as Charles Dewey, Samuel C. Sample, John S. Newman, all of Indiana, and Abraham Lincoln and Stephen A. Douglas of Illinois.

"The circuit-riders as a class were uneducated men who made up in industry and zeal what they lacked in culture. Pioneers of the onward wave of civilization, perfectly at home in the cabins of the first settlers or the wigwams of the Indians; ignorant of books, adepts in the study of human nature, they combined as did the early Jesuits, the heroism of Crusaders with the fortitude of martyrs."

He noted especially the woebegone expression on the face of the prematurely-old wife of a settler in whose cabin he spent the night. In conversation with the head of the household that night after supper, he began to understand the reason for this look on the faces of most of the women of the West.

"I have been kinder a rolling-stone," the settler began, "but I am a good deal better off than when I started. I own eighty acres of good land, twenty acres cleared; a yoke of oxen, a mule, a cart, and some farming tools, and besides as good a rifle as you ever laid your eyes on. And then, we have all the time been peopling the earth, as the Bible says we ought to. We have eight children — two of the boys have gone to work in the city, and I reckon that the old woman is good for two or three more. It has been pretty hard on HER, but I" — straightening himself — "am as hearty as a buck."

The next morning after paying fifty cents for his lodging in the one room with a family of ten, and a supper of corn dodgers, fried pork, and a queer kind of tea, he started on his ten-mile ride to breakfast.

As he followed the Indian trails on the banks of the Wabash, his thoughts in this lonely place were of the men who frequented these trails — the circuit-riding clergy and lawyers. Their story-telling at night in the settlers' cabins must have provided Lincoln with many of his rare yarns. But where are the people to possess and cultivate this wilderness to come from? he asked himself. Of the waves of immigration to surge farther and farther west, past mountains and on to the Pacific Ocean, of railways to connect the two vast boundaries, he could not even dream.

Through Frankfort, Delphi, Logansport, South Bend, La-Porte, he followed the wilderness trail. As he reviewed this journey, he expressed regret "that the Indian race would soon disappear, leaving no record of their origin and no reliable record even of their own existence. While this is to be their fate, there is cause for national humiliation in the fact that their disappearance has been hastened by the vices, the cupidity, the injustice, the inhumanity of a people claiming to be Christian."

At South Bend, he met Dr. L. G. Thompson of Fort Wayne; he was persuaded by Dr. Thompson to come to Fort Wayne. He reached the elevated plateau at the junction of the St. Joseph's and St. Mary's Rivers on June 26, 1833. To him the site appeared picturesque and commanding. Anthony Wayne's stockade was still standing. As yet there was little to commend the place except the sturdy character of its early settlers. They stood out as remarkably intelligent, enterprising, farseeing, kind-hearted and generous men. These qualities were demonstrated to him many times in this community of neighbors.

He began his career with a Fourth of July oration. On July 6, the first issue of Fort Wayne's newspaper — Democratic — the *Fort Wayne Sentinel,* carried the account of this celebration which had been held on the Court House square. The first article set up in type was the immortal Declaration of Independence, read by William McCarthy, another young attorney.

The toasts on this occasion were to the Wabash and Erie Canal — "The grand contemplated thoroughfare of commerce — another great link that binds the splendid car of prosperity to the fortunes of a free and grateful people."

At the time of the first issue, W. G. and G. W. Ewing were selling dry goods and groceries, hardware, canalers' goods. S. Hanna and Company were in the same business, which was increased by the commission and forwarding business down the Maumee River. Lewis G. Thompson was selling drugs and "doctoring." His competitor was Benjamin Cushman. Smalwood Noel was acting as magistrate. Hugh McCulloch, Thomas Johnson, D. H. Colerick, Henry Cooper, Charles W. Ewing, William McCarthy were practising attorneys.

Samuel Edsall and Hugh Hanna, a brother of Samuel, were carrying on the carpenter and house joiner business, each on his own hook, after dissolving partnership in January of that year. Col. J. H. McMakin was landlord at Washington Hotel, southwest corner of Columbia and Barr Streets. Lucien P. Ferry was in the tavern business on the northwest corner of Columbia and Barr in the Eagle Tavern. Francis Comparet and Alexis Coquillard were Indian traders. Joseph O. Boggs was a schoolteacher and Henry Rudisill, postmaster.

It was noted that the northern mail was carried by the way of Niles in Michigan Territory, to Chicago twice a week; the western by way of Logansport twice a week, southwestern by way of Winchester once a week. Thomas Pritchard, described later as a heavy merchant of Portland, Oregon, was at that time painter, glazer and paper hanger. Henry Work and Nathan Farrand and Company were Boot and Shoe makers and tanners. John Spencer was receiver of public moneys (county treasurer today), and Robert Brackenridge was register (now recorder). Allen Hamilton was clerk.

After his speech, Hugh McCulloch was seized with a chill, followed by a long illness. He never ceased to be grateful to Dr. Thompson, his sister-in-law, Mrs. Forsyth, and a Catholic priest, not named, for the care they gave him. It was October before he was able to be about . . . "although little better than a skeleton, I took possession of a ten-by-twelve office which Dr. Thompson had built for me, and hung out my shingle as attorney-at-law. I had not long to wait for clients."

Such were the neighbors when Oliver Fairfield and his brother, Asa, both sea captains, came from Kennebunk, Maine, in 1834. Captain Asa brought with him $30,000 in cash, the largest sum ever brought into the community up to that time. Mrs. L. G. Thompson sewed the money up in a mattress for him. Later, she hid it in the false bottom of a small rocking chair. Alarmed for the safety of the money when some unruly Indians came into her home, she took a small child in her arms, seated herself in the chair, and proceeded to rock and pretend it was ill. As a matter-of-fact, she was pinching the youngster to make it cry and help to play the scene realistically.

Her audience seemed to be convinced, as they left her alone with her patient.

In October, 1835, McCulloch was appointed cashier and manager of the Fort Wayne branch of the state bank of Indiana, the eleventh to be established. The bank was started in the house owned by Francis Comparet on the south side of the first block of Columbia west of Calhoun at a rental of $200 per annum. The rear room and garden were occupied by Smalwood Noel, justice of the peace, at $5 per month. McCulloch remained cashier of the branch, later in its new location southwest corner of Main and Clinton, and director of the state bank until the expiration of the charter in 1857.

Miss Susan Mann and Miss Alida Hubble came to the village in 1836 from Plattsburg, New York, as the first women teachers in Fort Wayne. My grandfather Comparet remembered them as "competent teachers who did away with the rawhide and hickory gads that the male teachers had in their schools. They were successful and were well liked by their pupils of which I was one."

Miss Mann became the wife of Hugh McCulloch and Miss Hubble married Royal W. Taylor, merchant, from Glastonbury, Vermont. Thirty-five years later, Mr. and Mrs. Hugh McCulloch returned to Plattsburg, where they had been married, to observe their wedding anniversary.

During these Indiana banking years, the wilderness was so safe that Mr. McCulloch made the three-day ride on horseback unarmed from Fort Wayne to Indianapolis, carrying thousands of dollars in his saddlebags without the slightest fear of being robbed.

He considered that the real hard work of his life commenced with his selection to the presidency of the Bank of the State of Indiana, which began its career on January 1, 1857. This bank continued to prosper under his management until the outbreak of the Civil War. It was one of three banks in the country which was able to weather the financial storm of 1855 to 1857. He resigned this post to accept the Office of Comptroller of the Currency — a new bureau created by the passage of the national banking law. This meant the establishment of a new financial system by the government. It is believed that faith in Mr. McCulloch throughout the nation was such that his name restored confidence in monetary circles.

Better than most New Englanders, he was able to understand the story-telling Lincoln, who was often misunderstood by his contemporaries. Salmon P. Chase, Secretary of the Treasury during the Civil War, did not appreciate the jokes and stories which brought Mr. Lincoln so close to the hearts of the people, Mr. McCulloch states. Relations between the two men were never cordial. And yet in all fairness, Mr. McCulloch states his conviction that Mr. Chase's services next to Lincoln's were of the greatest value during these years from March, 1861, to July, 1864.

"Mr. Lincoln had no educational advantages in his early life," wrote Mr. McCulloch. "In appearance he was unpreposssessive, in manners ungraceful, in taste unrefined, or at least peculiar, but he was warmhearted and genial. In knowledge of men, in strong common sense, in sound judgment, in sagacity, Mr. Lincoln had no superior. He was unassuming, patient, hopeful, farseeing. He was also one of the bravest of men. In saying this I do not refer to personal courage, in which he was by no means deficient; but to bravery of a higher and rarer kind — bravery which was steadfast under criticism of his friends and the assults of his enemies.

"Throughout his administration, Mr. Lincoln was wiser than his enemies, wiser than his friends. Beside the attacks of his political enemies, to which he was indifferent, he was constantly charged by those who claimed to be friendly, with hesitation when hesitation was dangerous. They were, for instance, impatient at his tardiness in using his war power to free the slaves and they censured him without stint. He was troubled by this censure, but his purposes were not shaken by it . . .

"His aim was to keep abreast with public sentiment with which no man was better acquainted and not to go too fast to avoid the charge of going too slow . . .

"I never think of the manner in which Mr. Lincoln performed the most difficult and responsible duties which ever devolved upon mortal man; of the enormous labors which he performed, of his faith in the right, his constancy, his hopefulness, his sagacity and his patience under unmerited and bitter criticism, without feelings of admiration akin to reverence."

And yet, even Mr. McCulloch was nonplussed at times by Mr. Lincoln's apparent levity. Eight or ten days after the first Bull Run battle, he visited Washington. He was still head of the State Bank of Indiana. The city, he said, was in a panic. Members of Congress and civilians were in terror over the military situation. The next morning he called with a few friends upon the President.

"He received us kindly and tried to amuse us with anecdotes. I did not at that time know him well, and I was surprised that he should relate anecdotes when the government of which he was the head seemed to be in imminent peril. I have to confess that I left Washington in a very despondent mood."

Of his grandfather's banking career, Ross McCulloch told me, "He had the knowledge and the judgment. Those who wanted him, sold him on the national banking idea on the strength of the need of the Civil War to have bonds to finance it. Lincoln asked him to be Secretary of the Treasury which he did for patriotic reasons. This was his first post as member of the cabinet under three administrations — Lincoln, Johnson, and Arthur."

Hugh McCulloch's appointment as Secretary of the Treasury in Lincoln's second administration, following Fessenden's resignation, came about in this way, Mr. McCulloch wrote:—

"A day or two after his second inauguration, Mr. Lincoln requested me, by one of his messengers, to call upon him at the White House at some time during the day, which I did in the afternoon. He was alone, and as he took my hand, he said: 'I have sent for you, Mr. McCulloch to let you know that I want you to be Secretary of the Treasury, and if you do not object to it, I shall send your name to the Senate.'

"I hesitated for a moment and then replied: 'I thank you, Mr. President, heartily for this mark of your confidence, and I should be glad to comply with your wishes if I did not distrust my ability to do what will be required of the Secretary of the Treasury in the existing financial conditions of the government.'

" 'I will be responsible for that,' said the President. 'I will be responsible for that, and so I reckon we will consider the matter settled.'

"The President seemed to be greatly careworn, but he was cheerful and after a brief talk with him I returned to my office and said nothing to anyone about the interview. I was, I confess, gratified by being asked to take the most important place in the government, but I was troubled as I thought of the duties and responsibilities. I could not say which feeling predominated — gratification or dread. The next day my nomination was sent to the Senate, and was, I understand, unanimously confirmed."

In one of Mr. McCulloch's last conversations with the President, Mr. Lincoln said, "I am here by the blunders of the Democrats. If, instead of resolving that the war was a failure, they had resolved that I was a failure and denounced me for not more vigorously prosecuting it, I should not have been re-elected and I reckon you would not have been Secretary of the Treasury."

Lincoln't effective use of the word "resolved" marks his most important utterances, for instance, "The Gettysburg Address."

In a locked-box opened many years after Hugh McCulloch's death, was found a letter written to him by A. Lincoln, April 13, 1865, the day before his assassination. With the faded Lincoln letter lay the communication from Daniel Webster.

Hugh McCullough was one of the mournful group who stood at the bedside of their stricken chief on his last night. He had been carried to a house opposite the theater where the physicians, friends and cabinet members had already assembled when Mr. McCulloch arrived.

"All night we stood or sat by his bedside. Not a word was spoken except by Mr. Stanton who in undertones gave directions to guard the exits from the city, to prevent, if it might be possible, the escape of the assassins. Once only was the impressive silence broken, when Mrs. Lincoln came in, and kneeling by the bed, and clasping a hand of her unconscious husband, gave vent to her irrepressible grief in tones that pierced every heart, and brought tears to every eye. When she was led away, silence again prevailed, and it continued unbroken until seven o'clock in the morning when the death shade came over his face.

"It had been a sleepless night in Washington. The theatre in which Mr. Lincoln was shot was well filled, and consquently there were hundreds to spread the shocking tidings throughout the city. Houses were deserted; women as well as men flocked the streets, but there was little heard except the tramp of feet in the crowded thoroughfares. The feeling was too deep for noisy expression."

Hugh McCulloch was the last surviving man of Lincoln's cabinet of thirteen men. His death occurred on May 24, 1895. He had survived Lincoln thirty years.

II.

Some Famous Also-Rans

1

THREE TIMES — in three 19th century generations — the red carpet was rolled out to welcome Fort Wayne's favorite presidential candidates with open barouches. Editors waxed lyrical. Parades, torchlight processions, ladies' broom brigades, honored the great men: Stephen A. Douglas of Illinois, James Gillespie Blaine of Maine, William Jennings Bryan of Nebraska.

In one respect the three were alike. When the smoke of the torches had rolled away, when the votes were finally counted, these favorites of the local electorate were famous also-rans. The extravagant claims of partisan editors in the days when they burned their opposing candidates in effigy in the public square stand unmatched in the annals of campaign literature. It was an era when no holds were barred and slugging below the belt was the usual practice.

When Stephen A. Douglas came to Fort Wayne, October 2, 1860, in his canvass against the "Railsplitter of the Sangamon," a huge sawlog intended to represent Abraham Lincoln was flung into the St. Marys River. Only one protest against the political float was made, however. When the float challenging the "Black Republicans" halted before the house of a rabid abolitionist, his wife came out on the porch "most unwisely . . . and with angry words raised her fist against this provocation."

At sunset there was a hue and cry, "Everybody to the Court House." This time a straw figure of Abraham Lincoln was hanged in effigy.

There is no doubt that this was the most exciting campaign this country had ever seen. Big rallies were held everywhere. Placards annouced that on Friday, August 3, Gov. Willard of Indiana, Henkle of Goshen and Popgun Smith of Fort Wayne would be the drawing cards at Leesburg. One paper announced that Stephen A. Douglas of Illinois, Brigham Young of Utah and Blondin, the rope dancer of France, would be on the same program.

Dawson's Times — an independent paper in this community bearing on its masthead: "For President, Abraham Lincoln of Illinois; for Vice-President, Hannibal Hamlin of Maine" — gave the following account of the Douglas rally in Fort Wayne, Tuesday evening, October 3, 1860:

"On the morning of the second instant, about 3 o'clock, Judge Douglas reached here, and was received at the depot by a large crowd of noisy, disorderly men — the conduct of many of whom is by no means, a thing which an enlightened community can think of but to deprecate. Many persons arrived during the evening before from the country about — and in the morning the crowd began to swell faster, and continued until the arrival of the trains.

"The desire to see Judge Douglas was manifested by all parties, men and women — and that, added to the fact that in the rural districts seeding had closed, enabled all classes to spend the day in Fort Wayne. This threw into the crowd a number which was doubtless one-third Republicans, whose appearance and deportment indicated that they were not of the modern School of Democracy. About 11 o'clock the procession formed. And when formed was long and drawn out. When the front part had passed around town and reached Townley's corner coming west, a carriage containing Judge Douglas and some friends drove, meeting it from front to rear. It was greeted with cheers.

"The trains of the Railroads were not as large as expected. That from the west toward Plymouth only had 24 cars. On all roads only 70 carloads arrived — less than 4,000 persons. After dinner the crowd assembled near the Methodist college, on the east bank of the St. Mary's. The stand being near the river, the assembly fronting on the side hill above the east thereof, a place well selected and well adapted.

"Before Judge Douglas arrived, D. H. Colerick made a few remarks which were confused and virulent and pointless. . . . Then followed W. S. Smith, Esq. whose remarks though desultory were respectful and better timed. Then a fellow who lives about Northport, Noble County, assailed the editor, 'as if the people before him had come there to hear our opinions expounded by anyone at all, much less an ignorant man' . . . After this fellow come S. H. Buskirk Esq. of Bloomington, Indiana, and filled up the time in a feeble way, till Judge Douglas arrived, late in the day.

"The judge spoke one hour. Of his style it is sufficient to say that it is neither pleasing nor forcible. His theme would have been threadbare had it not been given so many new features . . It had not one feature of true statesmanship about it — it showed rather the character of stump oratorism than the platitudes and comprehensiveness of a statesman's mind — as if addressed to ignorant men, than to the sound minds of well-informed freemen — aiming to raise a furore for himself, and be carried by a swell-mob into power, than reach the highest hopes of a true statesman by the sober second thought of a people. It was full of embittered feelings not only toward the Breckinridge party, but towards the President Buchanan — even worse toward the Republican party, whose platform he misstated grossly.

"It was the effort of a man whose star of glory was setting in a cloud — Whose hobby horse was making a last effort in the race — not with the hope of beating but to keep from being distanced — and the responses he met from the crowd were not the paeans of praise coming from the hearts and originating in matured and well-informed minds in behalf of a great principle — but the coarse huzzas from mouths leading out from prejudiced, obscured, obtuse minds.

"He was a master of demagogue, playing with a people who would be honest, if they were left to dictates of their own sense of right, but who fell an easy prey to designing men, as innocence to the wiles of the artful and accomplished seducer. In a word, it is not a statesman's speech. And then the idea of a man who was honored with the colors of his party, as a candidate for president of the United States, going and stumping it as a county candidate, did not fail to strike even his warmest intelligent friends as out of character and intolerable — a dangerous because bad precedent — and not in accordance with the genius of our Republicn institutions."

As to the numbers of people arriving by cars and lumber

wagons, there was vast disagreement, depending on your politics.

Judge Douglas stayed at the Rockhill house and the belligerent editors commented, "The vulgarity and noise kept up on the streets before he arrived, and showed that whiskey was doing more for him than he can do for himself. It don't take much sense, knowledge or gentility to be a Democrat."

And yet when the torchlight processions were over and the bitterness had died down, on Monday, June 3, 1861, the same paper announced, "A Great Man Has Fallen, Stephen A. Douglas, aged 48 years, one month and 11 days." And even his political opponents were hushed. But Allen County had cast 3,224 votes for Douglas, 2,522 for Lincoln, 42 for Breckinridge, 32 for Bell.

Stephen A. Douglas   James G. Blaine   William J. Bryan

2

Twenty-four years after the Douglas campaign, on October 19, 1884, the triumphal approach of James Gillespie Blaine of Maine was announced in the Fort Wayne Sunday Gazette. "The Plumed Knight on his way to Victory enters Indiana. Grand reception at Ann Arbor where he addresses the University students. Impressing upon their minds the importance of the Tariff question."

In bold face type, the same issue carried an invitation by the Allen County Central Republican committee to all citizens of Northern Indiana, Northeastern Ohio and Southern Michigan;

to Republicans, Democrats and Greenbacks for Monday, October 20. "Hail! Hail! The greatest statesman of the age, J.G.B. — Germany has her Bismark, England has her Gladstone, but America has her Blaine. Shout ye crowds, roar ye artillery, ring ye bells, a blithesome greeting to our noble guest . . . "

A monstrous demonstration was planned. The train was to arrive at the end of Main street at 2:20 p.m. bearing Blaine, "the great statesman, forensic orator, the noble husband, the tender father, the friend of the martyred Garfield, the man who occupies a greater place in the hearts of the American people than any living man, the noble American of the Americans, our next President, James Gillespie Blaine of Augusta, Maine."

It was clear by then that Blaine was coming to town.

The parade was planned in five divisions and was to include "railroad men with their lanterns, visitors from Van Wert, including the Ladies' Glee Club, the Ladies' Broom Brigade and the plumed Knights in uniform; representatives from Toledo, South Whitley, Defiance with a Plug Hat Brigade, Warsaw, Kendallville, Auburn with their Broom Brigade, LaGrange, Lima, Ind.; Huntington, Wabash, Andrews, Garrett, Wolcottville, Rome City, Albion with a Magnet Club, Pierceton, Arcola, Angola, Bluffton, Pleasant Lake, Fremont, Decatur. Bands were a cornet band from Ossian, a Ladies' Band from Andrews, and Sheldon, St. Joe, Monroeville, Aboite Center and Hoagland."

Magnetic Notes appeared at the end of the editor's flowery effusion: "Democrats are crazy with delight, the Andrews band are fine musicians and elegant ladies, twenty young ladies very handsome, too, will be here from Huntington, Mr. Blaine will speak both afternoon and evening from the Aveline House balcony. Mrs. Younge will act as chief of Sullivan's staff and will wear a gorgeous habit — heading the local equestrien committee. The Fort Wayne Young Ladies Broom Brigade will be a striking figure in the Blaine reception parade today."

And if you want to know what the well-dressed locomotive wore that day, I can tell you that, too. Wabash engine 1041 was magnificently and appropriately decorated: on the headlight a picture of James G. Blaine surrounded by a wreath of flowers; on each side of the cab, portraits of both candidates decked with small flags and natural flowers: in the sand box a fine flag; in front a number of small flags; front braces decked with bunting. The engineer was E. L. Tenney and the fireman H. C. Lenheim.

"Promptly at 2:30 standard time, the train consisting of Mr. Blaine's palace car Dakota and a luxurious Wagner car, dashed up the crossing and as the excited crowd saw Mr. Blaine at one of the windows a deafening shout went up." Three quarters of a mile of solid delegations and cheering citizens had tramped joyfully out to meet him.

"With him was a committee who had gone as far as Auburn: Judge Morris, the Messrs. Harper, Purman and Fairbanks. He alighted and was conducted to his barouche and took his seat. Then he read a handful of telegrams that had been thrust at him. Four vehicles carried the Blaine party which consisted of Major McKinley, Robert P. Williams and George M. Hipple. An escort line of citizens forming the Brown Hat club flanked the chief carriage. Women smiled, babies crowed, handkerchiefs fluttered, young ladies cheered.

"Peter Smyser had his grounds most beautifully decorated, and a huge transparency hung across the street — 20,000 for Blaine and Logan. Mr. Blaine smiled at these signs of loyalty and bowed from side to side to the innumerable ladies who lined either side of the street.

"There was one pitiful Cleveland and Halpin transparency on Berry Street and the boys shouted Rats as they passed under it. Every house on Berry Street was decorated — some more some less . . . Directly following the carriages was a hack containing four young ladies beautifully attired in white tulle and spangled over tin foil. Their head-dresses were made of silk bunting and were most artistic . . . The Misses Frank Tait, Clara Bowen, Ella French and Mrs. L. K. Eaton . . . Perhaps no feature of the parade was so much admired as this."

Somewhere around the Court House, the editor had to admit a counter demonstration suddenly took place. The Huntington boys who carried a much exhausted rooster labeled "Ohio," may have inspired it, he thought. From the moment the speaker was introduced by Judge Taylor on the Aveline Hotel balcony, pandemonium broke loose. A clown cut an antic upon some old lumber in the south entrance to the Court House; then some rude fellows in the crowd had a dispute. "Who hung two Irishmen in Buffalo?" "'Cleveland," "Who was it that put a widow lady in an orphan asylum?" "Cleveland." "And who trampled the workmen under his feet?" Again, "Cleveland."

On the suggestion of the Democratic chairman, the speakers and crowd en masse adjourned to Library Hall, "leaving the clown to tumble his flipflops on the Court House steps."

In conclusion, the editor commented: "We had a parade last night, which is why we smile this morning. We heaped the last straw on the Democratic back and it broke. It did for a fact. It is thought that possibly the Democrats will be surprised considerably in the next three weeks. By the way the Democrats did have some kind of a mob fooling around the back streets last night. They had an Ohio mugwump blowing off steam somewhere else.

"There is a general feeling that the gent who ran the mugwump rally had better return to the peaceful occupation of steering a bobtail horse and a sulky plough around a stump. As a political manager he is a dire failure, but might succeed as a wood-chopper. Notes — We whooped it up. It was Blaine day. They were bowled over. Democracy is shovelled into the ash-barrel. Democrats are like pounded ice — not what they are cracked up to be. We heard a Patriotic lady say 'I could just kiss them all.' And about 50 or 60 were wondering just what she meant!"

And for days the political column bore the heading, "Why We Laugh."

"Nov. 6 — Beyond doubt the election of Blaine and Logan.

"Nov. 10 — The anxious seat has 50,000,000 people on it.

"Nov. 17 — As it is now believed, after the fourth of next month the Democracy will be held responsible for the management of governmental affairs, etc."

Cleveland was our next President — the only Democratic President from James Buchanan, 1860, until Woodrow Wilson in 1912.

3

A routine check of a hotel register by a young reporter for the Fort Wayne Journal in August, 1896, was the beginning of the Bryan story in Fort Wayne. For the big name on the register was William Jennings Bryan, "boy orator from the West," who at thirty-six had just caused a stampede and captured the Democratic nomination for President of the United States at the Chicago convention in June.

Wild and very woolly were the scenes in the convention that day in Chicago, when Bryan and Pitchfork Tillman—according to the papers — took the reins away from Altgeld and started to run things.

The local reporter was the late Harry M. Williams who promptly called upon the Great Commoner in his hotel room, then rushed out into the street to corral some Democrats and rectify the omission of a reception committee who had failed to greet him when he arrived at the Nickel Plate station at 6 o'clock that morning. The first prominent Democrat he met was Judge Samuel Hench, a Civil War veteran, who was also a very impressive figure on a white horse. Both qualifications served to put him at the head of the great parade on Bryan Day in Fort Wayne, which was to follow in October.

Bryan's speech at Robison Park in August has been lost among the records of his later appearance in Fort Wayne on October 22, 1896. The weather, we are told, was perfect. The special train bearing Bryan arrived at 8:20 o'clock in the morning over the Lake Erie and Western. He had spoken at Bluffton and Ossian, and made many brief appearances on the rear platform of his train. So his fame in this region was ringing from many throats as the booming of cannon announced his arrival.

Moreover, his speech before the assembly in the Democratic Convention will live forever in the annals of political history. "You shall not crucify mankind upon a cross of gold" were the impassioned words that captured the imaginations of men and won him his enthusiastic following.

And when the boy orator sat down amidst a crowd gone wild with enthusiasm, there followed a demonstration that lasted fifteen minutes. Boy Bryan they called him! "William J. Bryan, the precocious child orator, captured the Democratic Party," the press said. He was born on March 19, 1860, just before the outbreak of the Civil War. And among his warmest friends and admirers for many years were those same boys in blue who were young men at the outset of that struggle.

Newspapers were full of both praise and condemnation of Bryan. The mountain had labored and brought forth Bryan— a pygmy politician, some of them said. There were certain facts however, on which all agreed. "He never smokes, drinks, swears nor chews — and his language is pure. His voice is strong enough to be heard by thousands. And his appearance is a passport to the affections of his fellowmen."

Then the writers delved into history and brought forth facts about the great men who had just missed the presidency. Among them were Aaron Burr, John C. Calhoun, Martin Van Buren, Blaine, Butler and Webster. The presidential lightning they said, was the most eccentric form of electric energy known to either science or religion.

Well, then, with all this acclaim behind him — with the plaudits of the multitude in that Chicago convention ringing in his ears — he started out to win his way eastward. And one day the paper stated that "The Hon. William Jennings Bryan of Nebraska today made a grand stride out of the west toward the heart of the enemy's country. He crossed Indiana, Ohio, spoke from the back of his train, stopped at Monroeville, Rome City and many other towns around, shook hands with men, woman and barefoot children."

"Tickled — just as pleased as a boy with a pair of red top boots — because the New York paper printed his speech at Madison Square Garden," were the headlines of a local paper about that time. On August 2 he spoke at Robison Park. And on October 22, 1896, came Bryan Day in Fort Wayne!

The weather was perfect. The railroads furnished low rates. And people flocked into town from all over the county. Bryan's supporters wore silver ribbons in their coat lapels for Free Silver, the battle cry of his campaign. Sixteen to one! Some folks said that meant 16 kids to one vote. But 16 persons rode white horses in the big parade.

There were the ladies' drum corps and the men's drum corps from Angola. There was a uniformed marching club wearing gray derbies. When Bryan spoke from the balcony of the Wayne Hotel, it is estimated that there was the largest crowd jammed into one block on Columbia Street between Calhoun and Harrison that this city had ever seen. The reporters for the Democratic press had to abandon their hack in order to hear the speaker.

"Some fellows in this community had five-foot faces that day," Judge Hench once told me.

The speeches were made from the Hotel balcony, Saengerbund Hall and the Princess Rink. The opposition paper said the crowd turned out for the parade because crowds always love a parade. Besides, there was red fire preceding it on the sidewalks.

This is the way he spoke: "I believe it was Cicero who said that if a citizen in a republic failed to do his duty he paid the penalty of having to live under the rule of worse persons than himself . . . My friends, if there is anything bad in our government, in the laws themselves, or in the execution of those laws, the fault lies with the people, because in this country people can have just as good a government as they desire."

The burden of his speech was this: "All that we ask is that we be permitted to have the honest, unbiased expression of the people of this country when they come to consider the question of this country . . . I want to talk to you tonight about a matter of business. Our opponents are all the time boasting that they have in their ranks all the businessmen."

Locally, Bryan was pictured as a family man in the best of standing, with three pretty, well-behaved children and a wife active in women's clubs out in Nebraska, who was a recognized leader in her home community. In fact, Mrs. Bryan had accompanied her husband on tour and while in Fort Wayne was presented with a hat made by Ora Seeney, man milliner about town. The hat — a theater hat of his own design — had a brim of silver tricotine edged with spangled braid, silver ornaments at the side, silver stick pins, a large bow of black peau de soie ribbon on the crown, with aigrettes coming from the center. The agreeable Mrs. Bryan even suffered her picture to be taken in the hat which she promised to wear the next time she went to the theater.

And when the all-important votes were cast and counted, it was found after the November election that Allen County had cast 9,909 votes for Bryan and 8,467 for the victor — William McKinley.

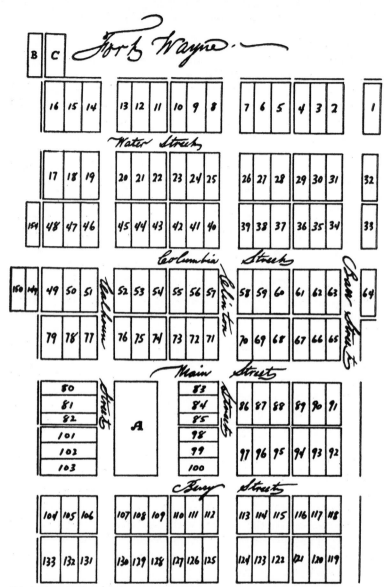

This is a facsimile of the original drawing of the Barr and McCorkle plat of Fort Wayne made for the proprietors by Henry Rudisill who afterward located here.

A. Public Ground for County Purposes, B. Burying Ground, and C. School lot. Lots No. 1, 32, and 33 are each 54 feet wide and 150 deep; Nos. 80, 81, 82, 100, 102, and 103 are each 51½ feet wide and 107 deep; Nos. 83, 84, 85, 98, 99, and 100 are each 51½ feet wide and 150 deep—the other lots are 60 feet wide and 150 deep. Barr Street from Columbia Street are 62 feet wide, and the same depth as the others. The alleys parallel with Water St. are 16 feet wide except those between 82 and 100 and between 85 and 98 which are 5 feet wide—The alleys parallel to Barr St. are 5 feet wide except those west of 80, 81, 82, 100, 102, and 103 which are 16 feet.

[24]

III.

From the Stump Up

IN THE FIRST place, our town, with its steepled symbols of many faiths, its tapestried yards and gardens, its parks, playgrounds and spacious market-centers for the sale of foods, clothing, and every gadget known to modern man, had to be built from the stump up without a bull-dozer.

It has been a hundred and sixty-five years since the very ground on which Fort Wayne stands could be called United States soil. The forty-acre military reservation had been the property of the United States only since the treaty of Greenville in the summer of 1795. The matter of building a town began after a survey, with a proclamation by President James Monroe for the sale of these government lands to the highest bidder at a minimum price of $1.25 an acre.

Clearing the land was therefor among the first of many problems that confronted the early settlers of Fort Wayne after the fort that had stood fully garrisoned for twenty-five years, was evacuated on April 19, 1819. In fact, THE TOWN — the original plat of Fort Wayne — was the object of many years of grubbing as well as planning, until the first city charter was drawn up by Franklin P. Randall in 1840.

For even a small town of 118 lots proved to be a formidable undertaking. And yet, the only way to avoid the grubbing was to use a big plow with five or six yoke of oxen. There was no easy way. It was strenuous labor for either man or beast. Nevertheless, our forsighted city planners could handle even the hardest manual labor.

On October 22, 1823 — the twenty-ninth anniversary of the dedication of the Fort — the lands about Fort Wayne not immediately adjoining the stockade were opened to public sale. From the land office set up in the stockade, Captain Samuel C. Vance, federal land agent, assisted by a young Irishman from County Tyrone by the name of Allen Hamilton, met the eager buyers who had come from far and near to purchase the choice lands.

In this area of scattered trees, broad swamps, sites of Indian camps at payment time, meandering springs, fortunes were made this day. The choicest plot of 118 lots was purchased by two men who came to the land sale down the St. Mary's River in a batteau carrying their luggage and specie. By combining their resources, they purchased what is known as the "Original Plat," at the minimum price. John T. Barr, a merchant of Baltimore, and John McCorkle, an enterprising young citizen of Piqua, Ohio, planned to have their plat laid out as business and residence lots immediately.

Sixteen blocks were included between the four north and south streets — Calhoun, Clinton, Court and Barr, and the five east and west streets — Water (now Superior), Columbia, Main, Berry and Wayne, in the original plat. The portion is designated as "the north fraction of the southeast quarter of section two, township thirty, north range east."

Immediately south of this area on which the original town was laid out, the south half of the southeast quarter of section two and the southwest quarter of section one — just east of the fort — were purchased by Barr and McCorkle.

The eighty acres of thicket and swamp directly west of the town plat were purchased by Alexander Ewing at $1.25 an acre and became known as Ewington — Ewing's addition.

Among the buyers in the fall of 1823 was William Rockhill who came from Burlington, New Jersey, and purchased a large tract to the west. Another large tract west of town was entered by Paul Taber and purchased by Tom Swinney, a young man from Piketon, Ohio, who later married Paul Taber's daughter, Lucy. The portion of Swinney's land lying on one side of the St. Mary's River was fertile for farming. On the other side, a wide prairie offered suitable grazing land for the ponies and mules Swinney planned to buy. Another large tract entered by Samuel Taber, a son of Paul, was purchased by William Rockhill.

The settlement at the time of the first land sale consisted of a few one-story log buildings collected about Clinton, Barr, Columbia, Lafayette and Water Streets. To the east and south of the fort, the ground was comparatively wild where it had been stripped of timber to build a fort. A wagon road wound among the second growth of scrub oak.

By September 18, 1824, when the first lots of the original plat were put up for sale, there were twenty-seven citizens on hand to buy the 36 lots. The entire sale netted $690.50, or an average of $20 per lot. So far it was a town on paper, but at least some of the stumps had been removed.

South of the stockade the soil was of unsurpassed fertility where the officers' gardens of flowers and vegetables had been the marvel of all beholders. Directly west of the stockade stood the two-story Council House of hewn logs among wooden buildings of an inferior sort.

Not until 1822 had regular mail routes been established to Fort Dearborn and the Ohio settlements over the only two trails. St. Mary's, the nearest of these settlements, was a hundred miles away. And yet, a village supported by the fur trade in deerskins, raccoons, bears, wildcats and foxes, had grown up. On flatboats and pirogues, on horseback, in wagons over uncertain trails, had come settlers and their families who had braved wolves, Indians, swamps, loneliness, and had remained.

On April 1, 1824, the state had formed Allen County, named for Colonel John Allen, a gallant Kentuckian who, after coming to the relief of besieged Fort Wayne in 1812, had lost his life in the battle of River Raisin, south of Detroit.

The names listed as buyers of the first lots sold in the Barr and McCorkle plat were: Francis Comparet, William Barbee, William Suttenfield, Edward Mitchell, Thomas Rue, Charles W. Ewing, Rees Goodwin, John H. Griggs, Mathew Griggs, Benjamin B. Kercheval, Christopher Valleynitte, Chief Richardville, Alexander Ewing, William Murphy, Benjamin Archer, Moses Scott, William N. Hood, Jacob Everly, Walker and Davis, Samuel Hanna, Moses Gerard, Abner Gerard, Henry Diehle, Benjamin James, Benjam Glassbrenner and Jacob Glassbrenner.

Land for the present Court House square was donated by the owners of the original plat at a cost to them of $500. A plot four rods square at the northwest corner of the plat was also donated by them "for a church, to be no particular denomination but free to all."

Masses were said in the Catholic homes until such a time as the little frame structure was built on the acre of land largely purchased for $100, July 1, 1831, for St. Augustine's church, site of the present Cathedral of the Immaculate Conception. Downeast Yankees and others of the sect most of them belonged to would build their first one-room church six years after their organization on July 1, 1831, of the First Presbyterian church. The white belfried structure stood near the corner of Berry and Lafayette Streets.

The stream of citizens continued to come during these early years from New England, Maryland, Kentucky, Ohio, Virginia, Pennsylvania, and New York State, to mingle with the best families of Detroit and Monroe, in Michigan Territory. The money they brought was Spanish coins — dollars, halves, quarters, eighths and sixteenths or 'levenpence — worth in York currency eight shillings to the dollar.

A dime was good for only two drams, while a quarter bought five drams of the best French brandy or old Dayton whiskey. Shrewd buyers were on hand for the opening of the first land sale to make the most of their opportunities and to secure for themselves all the land their means could afford.

If not the shrewdest, at least the most important to the largest number were the buyers of the Barr and McCorkle plat of 118 lots to be shared by individual citizens of a growing community.

The policy of Barr and McCorkle continued to be carried out by their resident agent, Henry Rudisill, 28 years of age, who arrived on Christmas Eve, 1829, in a carriage, with his family from Lancaster, Ohio. That policy was one lot to a buyer, and all lots to be laid out only as fast as those already laid out were disposed of. They were building a town, and they did not think it good policy to sell two or more lots of the original plat to a person even though the person wanted to improve them. After all, they might not improve them in such a way as to be of benefit to the town.

By 1825, with a population approaching 200, a log jail building was erected on the southeast corner of the public square. The upper floor was to be used as a debtor's prison. The construction of the building was such, however, that one notable character who found himself incarcerated there frequently, discovered that he could lift one of the logs, step out, and replace it.

A "County Seminary" provided for in the Barr and McCorkle grant was built of bricks on the west side of Calhoun Street, north of Water (Superior). John P. Hedges was the first teacher. About the same time, Henry Cooper, a lawyer, opened a school in the unused debtor's room of the jail.

The business area now began to extend west and south from the corner of Barr and Columbia. To the first Indian trading-stores open in the spring and fall were soon added a grocery, a tavern, hat shop, dry goods store, post office, drug store, lawyers' offices, carpenters and joiners, cabinet maker, brickyard, blacksmith, bootblack, draper and taylor, shoemaker, barber and silversmith. The pioneer butcher, Peter Kiser with saw and scales and giant cleaver no other man could wield, is remembered to this day.

Court days twice a year after 1824, and election day were noted for fights with fists and feet. The most difficult conviction to get according to the white man's law was murder.

The William Wells' pre-emption of 320 acres granted by Act of Congress, May 8, 1808, was entered by the heirs at the first land sale at $1.25 an acre. In the June, 1825, term of the Circuit Court, the heirs of Captain William Wells petitioned for the partition of the claim in the forks of the St. Mary's and St. Joseph Rivers. The partition in eight parts was made according to Wells' will. The attempted murder of his daughter, Ann Turner, by her brother-in-law, James Hackley, and his suicide, resulted from this court action.

Captain Hackley's portion was appromixately 21 acres on the north bank of the St. Mary's, in a line with Clinton Street, now part of Lawton Park. Mrs. Turner's nineteen acres was on the east side of Spy Run. When the division of the estate was made, a transfer of the two properties took place. Notwithstanding a mutual agreement made between the two to accept the court's decision, Captain Hackley refused to honor the agreement. When Mrs. Turner moved in with him, he became enraged and attempted to carry out a determination to take her life as well as his own. He succeeded in taking his own life.

The rate of county assessment on personal property for the year 1824 was: male person over 21 years old and upward, $37\frac{1}{2}$ cents; work oxen, three years old and upward, $18\frac{1}{4}$

cents; gold watch, $1; silver watch, 25 cents; pinchbeck watch, 25 cents; pleasure carriage, four wheels, $1.50; pleasure carriage, two wheels, $1.

With the incorporation of the town in 1829, a tax of two per cent was assessed on town lots. As hopes for the passage of the canal bill rose, values had increased. Henry Rudisill considered the corporation taxes high, until he was assured that considerable improvement was to be made in draining ponds, action which would add to the health of the place as well as to the convenience of the streets. Next year the tax would not be so high, he was told.

The Canal Bill passed and became a law early in 1830. The last of the lots sold at public sale had brought as high as twenty-six dollars in the last week of 1829. By April, 1830, Rudisill had received of Allen Hamilton a first payment on $75 for lots 71 and 72 on the southwest corner of Main and Clinton, to be sold at a modest price previously quoted by John Barr, one of the proprietors. Lot 76, present site of Riegel's, was sold to Hugh Hanna, a brother of Samuel, for $200. Rudisill made what he considered a fair bargain with two men to clear 18 acres of land in exchange for Town lot No. 29, on the alley on the South side of Water Street between Clinton and Barr, which he valued at $120.

The problems confronting the proprietors of the town are stated in the letters of Henry Rudisill to Barr and McCorkle, beginning January 2, 1830. With his family of four, he was living in two rooms for which he was paying a high rent. "I am very anxious to get out of the house we at present occupy. H - - - - keeps a rough house, it is a real brothel or grog-shop."

Labor, produce prices, rail timber, canal projects, sale of lots, clearing of land, and taxes were of the greatest importance. The grubbing of stumps was the most strenuous of many labors.

"I am pushing the clearing of land as fast as possible but find it a heavy job, so much grubbing," he wrote on January 16, 1830.

Repeatedly he urged the need for German immigrants because they were dependable and willing to work for less than Americans. "They will also make good citizens of a town . . . Their women are good in cornfields," he added. The most industrious and temperate are the Wurtemburgers, he stated. Moreover, he considered that three Germans were worth six of the common hands to be found here.

How to remit the money paid him — principally specie — was also a problem in the "Western Country," as they called Fort Wayne. One of the ways, Mr. Hamilton informed him, was to send their money to Detroit and procure drafts.

"Money is very scarce and all are complaining about the removal of the Indian payment," he reported.

The removal of the Indian payment of annuities from Fort Wayne to Logansport by General John Tipton, Indian agent, was believed by Rudisill and others engaged in business to be injurious to Fort Wayne. Chief Richardville was trying to have it brought back.

"Messrs H. & Co. (Hannah and Company) offered me a young man who has been doing business with them. His name is Wallace, brother-in-law to Lewis, at 100 dolrs a year. If you had no objections I thought of taking him for a while. The business here will not justify us in paying high wages to a Clerk and a young man who has been used to more active business would not content himself," was a part of the April 3, 1830 weekly report.

Wallace, brother-in-law to Major Samuel Lewis, Indian sub-agent at Fort Wayne, was presumably David Wallace, young lawyer of Brookville, Indiana, who had been named special prosecutor to the grand jury that met in Fort Wayne May 12 and November 10, 1828. He was the father of Lew Wallace, who had been named for his uncle Major Samuel Lewis, and is said to have been a frequent visitor at the home of his Aunt Katherine and Uncle Samuel in their double-hewn log house on the south side of Lewis between Clay and Monroe. The house and grounds were notable for a luxurious garden and roses that covered the house in summer.

At any rate, David Wallace represented Franklin County in the lower house in 1828, 1829 and 1830, at a salary of $2 a day. As Lieutenant Governor of Indiana in 1831, at the same pay, and Governor in 1837, he is said to have spent most of his time for several years astride "Ball" his $40 horse, on the way to and from his duties.

Major Lewis is credited with laying out the streets of Fort

Wayne south of Lewis Street, which was named for him, on lines conforming to the points of the compass. The streets laid out previously had accommodated the angle of the first houses built close to the shelter of the fort without regard for the true points of the compass.

The first addition to the original plat was made in 1830. At this time Congress authorized the associate judges of the circuit court to enter at the land office at $1.25 an acre for the use and benefit of the county, such a portion of the military tract of forty acres about and including the blockhouses and palisades of Fort Wayne and the reservation for the Indian agency as "may not fall under the canal act of Mach 2, 1827." By an Act of Congress of May 31, 1830, twenty acres of the west side of the fort reserve were entered by the county. Francis Comparet, county agent, was directed to borrow the money needed. Henry Rudisill provided the funds for the new county addition and the lots were offered for sale.

The second addition to the original plot of Fort Wayne was laid out in 1835 when Cyrus Taber purchased the remaining portion of the military tract about the Fort site, platted it into forty building lots as Taber's addition. This left only one blockhouse standing.

In all communications of Henry Rudisill with the proprietors of their plat, it was referred to as "The Town," with something akin to reverence for a promised land worth working for.

2

After sundown Christmas Eve, 1829, in the face of a stiff gale and within sound of howling wolves, Henry Rudisill stopped his tall closed carriage, drawn by a team of horses on what was to him an unfamiliar trail. Ahead were two postilions, acting as guides and escort. Their beards were frosted in the chilling air.

Within the snug curtains were his wife, the former Miss Elizabeth Johns, their three children — Henry, Frank and Elizabeth — and a nursemaid. They had been travelling for two weeks from their home in Lancaster, Ohio, over bad roads, where their progress had been impeded by water. It was growing late. The weird sound continued.

A child began to whimper. "Don't be frightened," said the eldest boy to reassure his sister, "it's only a steamboat."

The horsemen turned back to speak with "Captain" Rudisill. "We ought to be there by now," he said. "We must have missed the trail."

"Better stop where we are," 'Captain' Rudisill directed after a moment's thought. "If we missed the trail to Fort Wayne, we can't get back to it this night. Then we can start out fresh in the morning."

With no shelter but their covered carriage, they set up camp for the night. Christmas Eve in the wilderness! The men built a circle of fire to keep the wolves away. The children slept as happily as if it were Christmas Eve in their own little beds and they would wake to see the tree and all that Santa brought them in the morning.

And thus on Christmas Eve, 1829, as the story goes, Henry Rudisill, young pioneer, paused at the portals of the promised land. Morning broke fair. The horsemen who had kept watch by turns the night long, rode ahead into the village of Fort Wayne. For they had stopped on the Wayne Trace at the very threshold. They returned shortly accompanied by a number of citizens from the fort, who afforded an escort of honor the rest of the way.

Henry Rudisill was one of Fort Wayne's first promoters. Coming as the land agent for Barr and McCorkle, who laid out the first plat of the town, he stayed to establish a grist mill, a saw mill and a woolen mill.

The Rudisill Grist Mill, built by Henry Rudisill and his father-in-law, Henry Johns, in 1830 was the first one in this community equipped to manufacture marketable flour in northern Indiana. It stood opposite the present site of the electric power house on Spy Run Avenue, just below the State Street bridge. Across the road he built, in 1830, his stately residence which was for many years a spot of quiet beauty known to the entire countryside.

A few years later he put in operation the first machine for carding wool ever used in Allen County. The wool was brought in by the farmers for miles around.

As agent for Barr & McCorkle, he began his correspondence with his employers on January 2, 1830, immediately after his arrival with his family and goods. Like many another careful business man of his day, he preserved copies of his letters in a leather-bound book. This book is now in the possession of some of his descendants. It came to them from his daughter Miss Eliza Rudisill, the last of the original family, who had carefully expurgated many of the letters with a pair of shears.

"Aunt Eliza was afraid that grandfather's frank statements about some of his fellow citizens might fall into the wrong hands and cause trouble," Mrs. William Hahn explained.

While recuperating from a broken leg, Mrs. Hahn permitted me to read the remaining letters in the room where she was confined. The Hahn residence was one of three planned and built by Henry Williams architect and contractor. All three, the Hahn, Hanna Homestead, and Hugh McCulloch home, were constructed with a facade of large square pillars.

This is the way Henry Rudisill recorded his impressions of early Fort Wayne in writing to John T. Barr of Baltimore:

January 2, 1830

"I arrived here on last Sunday a.m. after a very unpleasant journey of two weeks. Roads were extremely bad and water high. Teams loaded with goods and furniture arrived a few days after me. They were detained a considerable time on the road by high water. We had the misfortune of losing one of our best work cattle on the road . . . I am well pleased with Fort Wayne and the country surrounding it, and the citizens appear to be very attentive and obliging to strangers.

"I called on Cooper and Hamilton . . . We are expecting the news of the passage of the Canal Bill. If that should happen so that the canal will go into operation next summer it will enhance the value of town lots very much. Fort Wayne has been incorporated and a tax assessed upon town lots. I have been informed that they valued town property very high and a tax of four per-cent put on.

"Mr. Hamilton has informed me that Mr. Henderson intended clearing and opening a farm on the opposite side of the river on your land. Some persons have destroyed a considerable quantity of fine timber. Rail timber is very high and scarce. I am about contracting with a person up the river to deliver me rails delivered at the landing. I am also about contracting with Mr. Hughes up the St. Joseph's for lumber. We could pay him principally in goods. I should like to have a small assortment of groceries. There is not a pound of coffee and sugar to be had in town.

"A small stock of groceries and a few other goods would be considerable advantage to us in trading for what produce we want. The last of public lots were sold last week at public sale. The highest lot was $26. I think it would be a good plan to defer selling until we hear of the fate of the canal. There were several persons applied to me for leasing pieces of ground in the neighborhood of the town for a term of years. I do not think it wuold be a good plan to do so. I can improve all that you want improved in a short time. And then if opportunity offers you'll be at opportunity to sell whenever you please. Corn is 50 cents a bushel. Produce is very high."

Later he wrote:

"I wish you would hire some Germans from Germany and send them out to me. German immigrants are frequently landing in Baltimore and would be glad of the opportunity. You can hire a good stout young man for $60 or $70 dollars a year. If you get whole families it will be better."

In letters that followed he referred to the canal bill which "is not dead but sleepeth." His careful correspondence all indicates that he planned wisely and well before making his decisions. On February 13 he wrote: "I would be very glad if you would permit me to put up a building to live by myself. I have to pay a high rent for the one I at present occupy and there are but two rooms in it. It is very uncomfortable and inconvenient and I would prefer to have a house not in Town but some place near the edge of it. In consequence of having work hands and stock about me, it will also be of great importance to have stabling and shelter for my work cattle. The winter is severe and cattle to be exposed to the storms require more feed by wasting it. Mr. Holcomb, the gentleman who owns the Tannery is anxious to have a lot adjoining it. It is not in the Town Plot. Immediately on the other side where the cabins stand, I should like to build for myself. It is convenient to running water, and out of the Corporation. The buildings might be so situated as not to interfere with the laying out of lots. It would also be the most central or convenient to the several tracts adjoining Town."

These projected plans were carried out in building his Spy

Run Avenue residence and grist mill.

Fort Wayne evidently impressed the ambitious young man favorably, for it is familiar history that he remained and left a trail of good works as a monument to his memory. He served as Postmaster eight years under Jackson's administration and three years as Commissioner of Allen County. It has been claimed it was his personal influence with the German settlers that made the Democratic party the ruling party in the county. He was a powerful force in establishing the Lutheran church.

His granddaughter, Mrs. Hahn, recalled the gristmill's huge grindstones, imported from France, that were destroyed when the mill was dismantled many years ago. They could have been used in the garden, she said regretfully. She remembered when wheat was hauled to the mill by wagonloads from the surrounding farms, and flour was sent as far as New Orleans by pirogue. Her grandfather used to accompany these loads on the trip.

With his son-in-law, Rufus M. French, he founded the woolen mill, which was later known as the French-Hanna Mills. Theodore Dreiser told me that his father, who used to set up woolen mills in various parts of the state, helped to set up this woolen mill before the Civil War. It stood between the canal and the river near the old Spy Run bridge.

General Lawton's father was a millwright in the Rudisill Mill. General Lawton as a young boy, went into Army service from the Rudisill Grist Mill. It stood on a beautiful spot on the St. Joseph River and was for years a show place for picnics and drives.

The homestead nearby was built in 1832 and had a garden facing the river which the members of the family loved to recall. It was terraced and planted with choice shrubbery. Peonies, roses, syringias, spirea, lilacs and many other varieties of plants and shrubs grew in profusion.

When Mrs. Henry Rudisill came to the village of Fort Wayne, there were friendly Indians nearby who brought baskets of berries to her back door. But as time went on and she told the Indian stories about their loves and hates over and over, the family all grew tired of the tales which have been lost to posterity.

Two of her many daughters — Julia and Maria — were

married in a double ceremony. The couples planned to go to New York on their wedding trip. In order to do this they had to travel by stage to Coldwater, Mich. So the service was scheduled to take place at 7 o'clock in the morning. As a matter of fact, the event has gone down in social history as unique. Mr. William Ewing, a friend of the family, vowed he wouldn't get up that early to see anybody married. Mrs. Ewing went on calmly making her preparations. When she was just about ready to start, her husband changed his mind, hurried on with his clothes and started to the carriage with his shoes in his hands.

The two daughters were Mrs. S. C. Freeman, mother of Mrs. Hahn, and Mrs. Rufus M. French. Elizabeth married a Mr. Townley, prominent merchant, an associate of Mr. French, and died at nineteen. Mrs. Hahn recalled that three of the eldest of the eleven Rudisill children — Henry, Martha, and Elizabeth — attended Rev. William W. Stevens' select school in the basement of the First Presbyterian Church in 1838.

In addition to the letters still remaining in the Rudisill letter book, I was privileged to read a choice family souvenir — a sort of Valentine series of illustrated letters written in February, 1859, to a "Miss Rudisill" by an un-named beau. Miss Rudisill was on a grand tour of Cincinnati and Washington, D.C. while the young gentleman languished in Fort Wayne.

The pen sketches of the young lady's band--boxes and carpet-bags, sleighing in February in the old home town, antique costumes to be worn at "an old folks' concert," fashionable patrons at a concert given by Piccolomini, and gaily attired skaters on the St. Mary's River, were among the lively subjects of the gallant correspondent, who closed his fanciful epistle with his young gentlemen bowing low as they doffed their stylish high hats.

IV.
The Grand Old Manner

1

AS POST-RIDER, delivering newspapers to subscribers over a scattered area; sutler, hauling provisions for men and horses by ox-team from Troy, Ohio, to the treaty with the Miami Indians at St. Mary's, Ohio, in 1818, young Samuel Hanna kept himself busy before he came to pioneer Fort Wayne in 1819 to establish the corner-stone of what his biographers call his "colossal fortune."

At twenty-two, strong and ambitious, he began in the new raw settlement by building with his own hands a one-story log house at the northwest corner of what became later Barr and Columbia Streets for the purpose of trading with the Indians. At this spot he rebuilt later the first structure as a one-and-a-half-story frame, and eventually replaced it with a brick business block.

This was the four-square foundation of the career built upon the resource and energy of a man who worked tirelessly from his days as agent for the American Fur Company in the little Indian trading-post, until 1866, when Fort Wayne's population was approaching the 30,000 mark. His business career spanned every form of transportation from the flat-boat days on the St. Mary's and pirogue days on the Maumee. The Wabash and Erie Canal, the Lima and Piqua plank roads, the Pittsburgh and Chicago Railroad from Crestline to Chicago, a distance of 280 miles, were propelled to completion by his Herculean shoulder.

By 1843, Mr. Hanna was able to say that he could travel to Indianapolis and return by way of Lafayette and "Anderson-town," and feed his horse at his own corn crib every night.

Briefly outlined, this was but a small part of Samuel Hanna's contribution to this community. As merchant, State Legislator, Associate Judge of the Circuit Court, organizer of the State Bank of Indiana, my brief could go on and on until it filled a book. I leave the rest to a definitive biography.

In fact, all I ever started out to do was to talk with Mr.

Hanna's only living child, Mrs. Fred J. Hayden, in the Hanna Homestead, on a beautiful fall day in 1929.

Now if there is anyone who thinks it is easy to extract reminiscences from the so-called older generation, just let them first catch the generation. If you call for an appointment in the morning, they are going out to lunch. If you try the afternoon, you are left high and dry about 4 o'clock while they go out to tea.

In fact the older generation is not what it used to be. I understand they used to be quite different. There was a time when an old lady was an old lady from fifty on. And she wore caps or a bow on top of her head to distinguish herself. But not today.

When it comes to hospitality, however, the older generation certainly knows how to dispense it in the grand manner. Having caught your older generation, several pleasant hours are ahead. Fireside stories, bedtime stories, Indian stories, true stories! In fact all of the tales that have delighted little children in Indiana as far back as the times when the first settlers came in covered wagons, pirogues, or on horseback, are retold.

The leisurely charm, the grand manner of the early days had been maintained in the Hanna Homestead, built on east Lewis Street by Judge Samuel Hanna in 1844. His only daughter, Mrs. Hayden, lived there most of her life.

"You have broken one of my playthings," she said one time to her housekeeper when one of the original panes of glass was cracked. A curious flaw in the old window-pane had fascinated her as a child. She would run her tiny finger over the flat bubble that marked the pane of glass on one of her mother's bed-room windows.

Mrs. Hayden thought the house had been built the same year as the Hamilton Homestead on East Lewis Street, where Central High School gymnasium stands today. The Hanna Homestead as we know it — originally a red brick house on a ten-acre farm — was contracted for with Henry Williams in March, 1844. The entire tract belonged to Israel Taylor, Mrs. Hanna's father.

As we looked out of the front windows, Mrs. Hayden indicated where the Hanna addition had extended — from Lewis Street on the south to Wayne Street on the north. "And there

Mrs. Laura Suttenfield, known as the "mother of Fort Wayne" and three of her descendants: daughter Mrs. Jane Barbour, right, grand-daughter, Mrs. Eliza Barbour Thompson, standing, Hattie Thompson, great-grand-daughter, in middle, (Mrs. Fred Mueller, Sea Cliff, Long Island.)

Mrs. Fred J. Hayden

Judge Samuel Hanna in foreground on walk of his home, now known as the Hanna Homestead.

is where your family's land began," she said.

It reminded me of something my grandfather Comparet used to say. Harmar had forded with his army to meet the Indians some three-fourths of a mile below the head of the Maumee, as the banks were too steep at any other place. Below the ford was a piece of bottom land extending one-half mile below where Harmar had forded.

"There must have been a battle there on this spot for I have followed the plough many a day and picked up relics of those days."

His father's land had included Harmar's battlefield on the Maumee.

Long before my grandfather's day, the Quakers were shown the place where Harmar's men were slaughtered in 1790 and listened to William Wells' account of the most historic places. This is what they wrote about their observations: "The long vista of history with numerous shallow graves and many evidences of mortality brought forcibly to the mind of Friend Hopkins these lines from Young's Night Thoughts:

'Where the dust that hath not been alive!
The spade, the plough, disturb our ancestor.
From human mould we reap our daily bread.' "

Photographs of Samuel Hanna and his family taken in the sixties show the house just as it stands today. Hundreds of people came yearly to see the old home — the only homestead of its era left standing in its original state — and "Grandpa" Hanna's wonderful garden.

However so much had been written about Samuel Hanna, the great pioneer, born in Scott County, Kentucky, October 18, 1797, of Irish descent, that Mrs. Hayden preferred to pay tribute to her courageous mother. She had noted that the women were not given much attention in the histories of the great community builders.

In the winter of 1822, Eliza Taylor came in a sleigh from her home in Buffalo, New York, to visit her sister, Mrs. Laura Suttenfield, known for three quarters of a century as the mother of Fort Wayne. Cold weather closed in and the roads became impassable, so that Miss Taylor could not return home. During her stay she met Samuel Hanna and they were married.

Mrs. Hayden had been told that her parents' first home, a

two-story weatherboarded log house at the corner of Barr and Columbia Streets, had been a hospitable stopping-place for many notable people travelling through the wilderness on their way to Vincennes. There were so few places for the traveller to stay in those days. Moreover, it was the pleasantest and warmest house they ever lived in, Mrs. Hayden had often heard them say.

"Father" John Ross, pioneer Presbyterian preacher of Kokomo, Indiana, was one of these travellers who walked through the wilderness and stayed at the Hanna home on his first trip through this section. He never forgot the kindness, and ever after accepted the hospitality of this pioneer couple instead of stopping at an inn.

The Indians at this time were very friendly and peacable, Mrs. Hayden recalled her mother saying, as she told them about this early home. There was a large fireplace for the entire household, guests and all, in her big bedroom. Her high post bed was fitted with curtains which she kept drawn so that she might retire without fear of being disturbed by members of the household in search of a comfortable place to sit.

Mrs. Hayden was born in a large frame house on the northwest corner of Berry and Barr Streets, where the family lived "in palatial style," according to editor John W. Dawson. She remembered the First Presbyterian Church standing near the corner of Berry and Lafayette, which was sold to the English Lutheran congregation, and later torn down by Charles McCulloch to build his residence.

The large Hanna Homestead on East Lewis Street was built to house a family of eight children, the eldest of whom was James Bayless Hanna, grandfather of Miss Clara Carnahan and Mrs. Creighton Williams.

Her mother was a very brave woman, Mrs. Hayden told me. One time she received word by telegraph at midnight of the serious illness of her husband who was serving in the State Legislature at Indianapolis. She started immediately in a sleigh along the towpath. When she reached Logansport, she was met by a "gentleman" who called her by name and gave her the message that her husband was much better. She continued her journey and stayed with her husband all winter.

The first home of the couple was across Columbia Street from her Aunt Laura and Uncle William Suttenfield who lived on the southeast corner of Barr and Columbia, in the first house to be built outside the fort. A daughter, Sophia Suttenfield, said to be the first of the white children born in the fort, in December, 1813, had a highly romantic and adventurous life, Mrs. Hayden observed, as she handed me a clipping from a local paper. Sophia Suttenfield became a prominent figure in the history of Texas right after the war with Mexico. The story is that she was married four times; that only her first husband died a natural death, the second in a duel, the third in a rebel raid of Quantrell's men. She visited Fort Wayne with her fourth husband, Judge James Porter, fifty years after she left as a girl of 18.

How important Mrs. Hayden was in linking early Fort Wayne with its later days can scarcely be realized. Samuel Hanna had come to Fort Wayne in 1819 at the age of 22, when the country was an unbroken wilderness for hundreds of miles around. He established a small store in a crude log structure and there laid the foundation of his great fortune. His daughter was reading "All Quiet on the Western Front." Her Woman's Club year-book was lying on the table beside her when I called on a fall day in 1929.

For a moment it was pleasant to hesitate over some of the old ways and compare them with our own; to be grateful for this stately, sturdy background; and to be reminded of it by someone who was a part of it.

Our roads, our railroads, the canal, were largely the result of the vision and energy of Judge Hanna. The material evidence of his spirit were still left. However, even the house and grounds and photographs failed to give an adequate picture of a man of his dimensions.

"The real brain of the Pennsylvania, Fort Wayne and Chicago Railroad was Samuel Hanna," Dr. Allen Hamilton, grandson of the pioneer Allen Hamilton, wrote me one time in a letter about the Fort Wayne he remembered. "He largely planned the road and brought it to Fort Wayne.

"The real station for the road was never to be on Lafayette Street. It was taken there only to join the canal. Mr. Hanna was a very brusque and arbitrary man who would never let anyone cross him. In talking it over with my grandfather he said the station must be near his, my grandfather's, house (site of Central High School today).

"My grandfather saw the town would grow south and urged the station to be at Pontiac Street. Judge Hanna said, 'Allen, if you won't have the station there I will put it in my yard.' My grandfather said, 'Well then you can put it in the barn.'"

The site for the station at the foot of Lafayette Street was donated by Allen Hamilton. Judge Hanna donated five acres of land for the shops.

Eliza Hanna Hayden, Judge Hanna's youngest child, represented many eras in her lifespan. As mistress of the Hanna Homestead, she gave me her recipe for the peach cordial she offered her guests. "Keep away from federal agents," her companion had written in the margin.

As the niece of Laura Suttenfield, she had given me a clipping which opened up a whole vein of Civil War adventures.

As the daughter of the family, she loaned me family photographs taken by John Shoaff, showing her father in long Prince Albert coat and wide black hat; and quaintly attired groups in the yard and summer-house — the scene of many conferences with dignitaries of the state and nation.

Of the great doings at the time of the completion of the Pittsburgh, Fort Wayne and Chicago Railroad, when the illumination in the Hanna Homestead could be seen for six miles, she said nothing. She had told it so often and always in the same words: that the basement windows of the Homestead were on a level with the steeples of the church and Court House, and for that reason the illumination reached so far, just like a light-house.

We talked about the great stairway and the native walnut railing as I touched its smooth surface, polished by many hands. I walked through the spacious hall and down the pleasant walk that had led so many guests to waiting carriages. However, at the sound of a jangling bell, I was jarred sharply out of the past and into a street-car that did not belong to the history I had just been steeped in for an hour or so.

2

It would take a fortune-teller equipped with a crystal ball to come up with the truths that prove to be stranger than fiction.

If Laura Suttenfield had been told that a great grand-daughter of hers would marry the great grandson of an Indian squaw, she would have been skeptical to say the least, even if the Indian in question was Sweet Breeze, daughter of Little Turtle and wife of Captain William Wells.

As proof of such an imaginary prophecy, I offer the four-generation picture of Laura Suttenfield and three of her descendants, Mrs. Jane Barbour, Mrs. Eliza Barbour Thompson, and little Hattie Thompson, the donor of this picture. Hattie Thompson Mueller's collection which was sent to the Allen County-Fort Wayne Historical Museum in 1953, included her mother's silver tablespoons bearing the initial E for Eliza, silver butter knives and a napkin ring; an ivory miniature of a young officer in a Revolutionary uniform, and a packet of 49 letters from her husband's — the Wells' — family.

The letters had been written by members of William Wells' family — children, nieces, brother, grandchildren — from Kentucky, Fort Wayne, and Indian Territory. They had been prized by Oliver Farrand, great grandson of William Wells and husband of Hattie Thompson, the child in the photograph, who had preserved them after his death in 1921. Others before him had prized them too, enough to tie them with a strip of bright print that looked like the binding of a homemade waist, all wrapped in a needlepoint bag wearing the initials M. W., which I interpreted as the initials of Mary Wells, fourth child of Wells by his Indian wife.

The first letter had been written in 1812 by Oliver's grandmother, Rebecca Wells, from Lexington, Kentucky, where she was attending school, to her older sister Ann, in Fort Wayne, the wife of Dr. William Turner, post surgeon. The last letter had been written to Oliver Farrand by Mollie or "Sis" Hackely, a cousin, in Lawrence, Kansas, and implored him to watch out for Quantrell's men who were raiding along the border. Since Lawrence, Kansas, was the town Quantrell's men left a town of widows and orphans on August 21, 1863, and her letter is undated, the saga ends on a note of mystery.

To me there is something touching in the little packet of intimate and tender messages, especially the school-girlish communication written by Rebecca Wells in an excellent hand in which she mentioned her father's tragic death in the Fort

Dearborn massacre just a few months before.

"I am learning Spelling, Reading, Writing, and Arithmetic, Grammar, and Music, and will shortly begin Geography, these are the sciences our dear deceased Father wished for me to learn; in one of the letters to me, these are mentioned, and I with pleasure make them my study."

Young Rebecca, in a strange world, poring over her lessons in obedience to her dear father's last wishes, is quite a moving figure.

Later references are made by Ann Wells Turner to Major John Whistler, his wife and step-daughters, Governor Lewis Cass, the Suttenfields — not entirely flattering — Hannas, Kerchevals, General John Tipton, and others prominent in the life of the old fort before 1819. "Wellsington" near Fort Wayne, written in a beautifully shaded script, was the heading on letters from the Wells' family living in the fork of the St. Mary's and St. Joseph's Rivers.

Oliver Farrand was the son of Rebecca Wells Hackley's daughter, Ann Hackley Farrand, and Nathan Farrand, Boot and Shoe Maker and Tanner, whose name appears in early business records of Fort Wayne.

"Oliver Farrand was my husband," the Hattie of the photographs wrote me, "but I was never sure of his age. He claimed the records of the family were destroyed by fire. When we were married in 1903, he gave his age as 'over fifty.' Later he said he gave 1838 as the year of his birth to the insurance company, but was not sure whether it was right or not. His death occurred Nov. 15th 1921.

"He came to New York in 1866 and went into the jewelry business. Of his family he told me his mother (Ann Hackley, grand-daughter of William Wells) was widowed at 23 years of age with five children . . .

"Mr. Farrand had a miniature which he prized and which I sent out to the Museum. I believe it was a portrait of Captain Jack Hackley."

The miniature is of Captain James Hackley, Oliver Farrand's grandfather.

The signature is that of Hattie T. Muller, remarried and again a widow, living in Seacliff, Long Island.

The second letter of Hattie Thompson Muller was in reply

to my request for a photograph of Oliver Farrand. No photograph was available, she informed me; but continued with such information as she could supply. "If I remember rightly, Oliver told me Wm. Wells' wife was a daughter of Little Turtle. Am afraid I did not take as much interest in his family history, as I should have in those days.

"When you first mentioned a man in Louisiana was writing about a Suttenfield daughter, I knew it must have been Aunt Sophie, as she went south when a young girl. Mother spent a winter with her when I was a little girl, and I remember a story she told mother of having some sort of a government contract, she had a lot of gold coin and when she feared the Yankees were coming to her plantation, she put that gold in buckets, poured tar over the tops, strung them under her wagon and took her slaves further south where they would be safe. I do not understand the yarn, as Aunt Sophie had become a real southerner and detested the Yankees. She had plenty of Confederate paper money when the war ended, and always believed Lincoln would have redeemed it had he lived . . . "

As to Aunt Sophia and her adventures, she was selected for a biography by a man in Shreveport, Louisiana, for reasons outlined in a letter to me in 1951: "We became interested in doing this biography when we learned that she was such a colorful character who had known and lived through the experiences of Texas and had been close friends to the state and many national leaders. Such people as Robert E. Lee, Grant, Albert S. Johnson, and many others were guests in her plantation home on Red River near the present town of Denison, Texas. We have no intention of trying to . . . produce a sensational piece. She was a charming, vital individual who lived through and in the middle of a dramatic time in history."

The clipping handed to me by Mrs. Eliza Hayden proved of value to the biographers who expanded their plan for Aunt Sophia's story to me some months later with some corrections.

"Sophia did not lose her first husband by death. They came to Texas in July 1835, and obtained a grant of land for a little over 4,400 acres in what is now Houston County. Within a year, Aughinbaugh, her husband, departed for unknown places, one source said Mexico then to California . . . Eighteen years later someone returned and sold the land. The person who signed for the land had to make an X for his signature. I am sure that was not Sophia's ex-husband as he was a school-teacher in Fort Wayne . . ."

My correspondent is right. A receipt for tuition in Writing, Arithmetic, Grammar, Geography, dated Fort Wayne, Feb. 13th, 1833, signed with a flourish by "J. A. Auginbaugh," was loaned to Bert J. Griswold, by Mrs. A. J. Detzer and appears on P. 305 of Griswold's Pictorial History of Fort Wayne.

"A newspaper story stated that when she was 17 she eloped with a German army officer. My suspicion is that Aughinbaugh came to Fort Wayne from central Pennsylvania as that is the only place I found his name in the 1790 census as a school teacher . . .

"Sophia's second husband was Holland Coffee. The evidence seems to indicate that she married him in 1837 according to the early Texas manner, either a verbal or written bond . . . Holland Coffee was a member of the Third Congress . . . Sam Houston was there and danced with the bride.

"In 1846 after Coffee had built her the finest home about nine miles above the present town of Denison, it is said that James Galloway was dancing with Sophia and made some teasing remark . . . She became annoyed (which she could do) and demanded that Coffee horsewhip Galloway. The story is that he tried to get out of it . . . but Sophia demanded that he fight for his honor. They fought with knives and Coffee was killed.

"George Butt, an aristocrat from Virginia, was next. They were married by 1850. She was much impressed by his dignity and polished manners, but the natives disliked the same thing about him especially his superior manners. Quantrell and his men camped on Sophia's plantation (by this time she had several thousand acres) and one day George Butt went to Sherman to sell some cotton, Taylor, one of Quantrell's men, killed him and took the money and watch. Days later he was found, and Quantrell's men were still visiting now and then in Sophia's home. She recognized the watch and had Taylor arrested. They shot their way out of jail, but the complete gang never operated as a unit again. That was the breaking-up point.

"She married James Porter in Waco (she had gone there because things were getting too hot on Red River) in 1865.

He was on his way from Missouri to Mexico to get his fortunes rebuilt. Burleson, president of Baylor University, performed the marriage ceremony. She joined the Methodist Church in 1868. Although she taught Sunday School, she never seemed to be able to throw herself completely into it . . .

"In 1866 she visited Fort Wayne . . ."

Thus endeth the saga of Sophia Suttenfield, up to the point where her cousin's (Mrs. Hayden's) clipping took up her visit to Fort Wayne. The conventional four-generation picture of Laura Suttenfield and three of her descendants gives a fairly good idea of how these ladies wore their hair, and the clothes they wore, in an era that projected its fantastic adventures far beyond the enclosures of the Old Fort.

Sophia Suttenfield returned to her old home as one who rated newspaper space in tribute to a life of heroic adventures.

The Fort Wayne Daily Gazette for September 19, 1886, added a few more statistics to the record:

> Judge James Porter, at Preston Bend, near Denison, Texas, died Sept. 10, 1886, aged seventy-seven years. Judge Porter will be remembered by some of our oldest citizens as a son-in-law of the venerable Laura Suttenfield, of our city. Mrs. Porter, who survives him, was born where this city now stands, in 1815, in the old fort.

Jesse L. Williams

V.
Young Pioneers

1

WHEN JESSE L. WILLIAMS, twenty-four, came to Fort Wayne as chief engineer of the Wabash and Erie Canal, he had made a choice of three important positions. At seventeen he had already had his experience on the Miami and Erie Canal from Toledo to the Ohio River. At twenty-one he was in complete charge of a section of this canal. At the same time he had the chance to superintend the construction of the state buildings at Columbus, or come to Fort Wayne as chief engineer of the Wabash and Erie Canal. He chose to come to Fort Wayne.

Jesse L. Williams, grandfather of the late Creighton Williams, came to Fort Wayne in 1832 when the opportunities for an enterprising young man of twenty-four were almost unlimited. "I have always thought he did more actual work in Indiana than any other man," was the comment of Dr. Allen Hamilton, cousin of Creighton Williams.

It was a time when a great nation was engaged in the job of solving its traffic problems. It was extending its waterways, those arteries through which the life blood of trade was destined to course throughout its system. Its natural rivers and streams were being augmented by canals. In other words, the canal era was being ushered into our national life. History tells us that this era lasted from 1817 to 1837. It began with the building of the Erie Canal which helped to make New York what it became eventually, America's leading metropolis. It was ended with the national panic in 1837.

Like all great national enterprises, the canal era offered a challenge to young manhood. It was a great thing to be an engineer in the canal days and to have a part in the building of a nation. It was a part of the great American plan of Henry Clay, the plan for internal improvements. It was a plank in the platform of young Abe Lincoln when he made his first political race for office, as candidate to the state legislature from Sangamon County, Illinois, in 1832. The continuation of this plan for internal improvement was the first thing in Lincoln's mind when the smoke of battle had cleared away and the burden of the war had been lifted from his brooding brow.

Fort Wayne occupied a strategic position in this great canal project. It was the starting point of the Wabash and Erie Canal which extended south and west to Lafayette and north to Toledo, forming a link in a continuous waterway from the Great Lakes to the Mississippi, and thus from the Atlantic to the Gulf. It took the greatest minds of the time to conceive and execute these canal projects. The invention of machinery made later and more gigantic projects possible.

The young engineer was born in North Carolina in 1807 of Quaker parentage. An ancestor, Judge Lynch, founded Lynchburg, Virginia, for whom that place was named. He is fully as well known according to tradition, for having given his name to a law, Lynch law, a mechanism of frontier justice which civilized men are now agreed has no place in our present social organization. It was an outgrowth of conditions which have passed completely and that the noted jurist would have been the first to recognize as obsolete.

Those were lively days down on the Ohio. The young engineers must have been considered great catches by the young ladies of that day. Men dressed rather gaily as you may recall from pictures. They probably cut quite handsome figures in their tight-fitting buff-colored trousers and blue coats with fancy buttons. The change to severely plain attire for men which the French Revolution had made popular, had been a gradual one. There was still enough left of vanity in the sterner sex to allow rather gay attire. There were many romances during the canal days. Not that clothes make the men — but they sometimes help.

Mr. Williams brought his bride along with him when he came to Fort Wayne. He had been married to Susan Creighton in Chillicothe, Ohio, the year before. He had even made quite a sacrifice for her. That is to say, he had been read out of the Quaker Church for marrying a non-Quaker. Yes, you have guessed it. Creighton Avenue was named for Susan Creighton and Williams Street was named for Jesse L. Williams.

At the risk of repeating a tale too-oft repeated, I must relate the traditional account of the couple's first meal in Fort Wayne. They arrived on horseback shortly after their marriage and stopped first with Mr. and Mrs. Marshall Wines. The one-room log house of Mr. and Mrs. Wines near the present Spy Run was divided off for a bedroom by curtains made of bed quilts. Privacy for guests was arranged in the same manner.

For the first meal she served her guests, Mrs. Wines had only a kettle in which to boil water and a skillet with three feet and a tightly-fitted cover. She hung the kettle with water on the crane which swung in the large fireplace over the glowing logs. That was for the tea. The potatoes were put to bake in the hot ashes. Then she took her skillet and stood it over the hot coals. First she made and baked her biscuits, took them out and set them aside on the hearth to keep warm. Next she cooked the corn, and lastly the meat which was venison.

"The meal was then ready to serve and we know it was served with the sauce of that genial hospitality so well known of Mrs. Wines," was the way Mrs. Martha Brandriff Hanna retold the story as Mrs. Wines had related it to her.

Susan Creighton was the daughter of William Creighton who was in Congress during the war of 1812. During her father's absence in Washington she had come under the influence of the temperance propaganda, a terrible thing for the daughter of a traditional Virginia gentleman as it proved. For during his absence she confiscated all of his fine liquor. Later William Creighton was the first Secretary of State from Ohio.

Even more interesting in the family history of Mrs. Jesse L. Williams, is the fact that her grandfather, David Meade, entertained LaFayette at his estate, Chaumier du Prairie, near Lexington, Kentucky. The house was a show place for many years and is standing at the present time. He and his brother had gone from Virginia to England in their youth. They had lived with the grandfather of William Makepeace Thackeray, the novelist, and had attended Harrow School. They are even supposed to have been the originals of the young heroes in Thackeray's novel, *"The Virginians."*

So that is a part of the background of the youthful engineer and his bride who were destined to cast their fate with the enterprising young State of Indiana and the City of Fort Wayne. In 1834 when the canal surveys were authorized in Indiana, Mr. Williams was made chief engineer of the Indiana canal system.

From then on he lived in Indianapolis for seven years. On his return in 1840 the railroads had made some headway west of the Alleghanies and the canal project was at a standstill for lack of funds.

Building a canal through a wilderness was no child's play, although they were little more than boys in years who did some of the work. Mr. Williams, during his work on the Indiana Canal, traveled 3,000 miles during four months in 1838, mostly on horseback. It took not only knowledge and skill, but a powerful physique to withstand such rigors.

It is no wonder that the faces of these men in maturity wore a grim, determined look. They had dealt with life in the raw. They were disciplined in a school of experience such as we shall never see again. For the frontiers have disappeared. In one century such progress as the builders had never dreamed of has come to pass. There was only one railroad in the New England States when Mr. Williams started on his commission to build the Wabash and Erie cannal. When the canal-building project was at an end he continued his service to the state and nation in the building of railroads.

There were many new business ventures which required enterprising young men in Fort Wayne in those days. Jesse L. Williams went into business with Pliny Hoagland and Allen Hamilton in a grist mill at the corner of Clinton Street and the canal. He was associated also with Hugh McCulloch and Allen Hamilton in banking. The three men founded the Hamilton Bank.

Jesse L. Williams was a close friend of Abraham Lincoln. His work as chief engineer of the Fort Wayne and Chicago division of the Pennsylvania Railroad was the first of his railroad-building projects. In 1864 he was appointed by President Lincoln to the position of governor director of the Union Pacific Railroad. He held this commission under three presidents.

Every great engineer has a special gift of some kind. Mr. Williams always believed in selecting land that was on a low grade for the laying of rails. He recommended an unvarying maximum grade not to exceed 90 feet per mile, throughout the construction of the Union Pacific road which was to meet the road coming from the west at Ogden, Utah. His reports, which were presented to Congress, became the basis for a congressional investigation which led to the Credit Mobilier investigation. His report of the total outlay of funds necessary for building and equipping 1,100 miles of railroad meant a saving of nine million dollars to the Government and led moreover to the investigation which was one of the great financial scandals of that era.

Mr. Williams also opened up 200 miles of the Grand Rapids and Indiana Railroad, having been appointed receiver of that road in 1869. Here the character of the man was demonstrated once more. The time for building the road was limited and it was necessary for gangs to work day and night in order to finish the work in time to save the land grant which was due to expire in a short time. Mr. Williams during this period used to get up at four o'clock every morning until the work was completed. And it was completed due to those strenuous efforts just eight days before the land grant expired.

In his later years Mr. Williams never relinquished his active interest in affairs of the state and nation. His canal activities continued throughout the entire history of this era until the time when the canal was finally sold to the Government in 1876. His reports on the various routes through western mountain ranges, based on his actual knowledge of the territory, would fill several large books.

It was always Mr. Williams' staunch belief that our river water should not be used for drinking purposes. He had a lot to do with starting the local water works.

An interview which Jesse L. Williams had with Lincoln was the subject of a Lincoln story written in the July Scribner's in 1920 by Robert Brewster Stanton, son of the Reverend Robert Livingston Stanton, another friend of Lincoln's. They had met with the President in June, 1864, to discuss the coming Baltimore convention and disloyal preachers in Kentucky and Missouri.

When asked how he thought they should deal with the disloyal ministers Lincoln had answered his inquisitor in a letter to the effect that the government could not afford to run the churches. Mr. Williams had just returned from the general assembly of the Presbyterian Church of Newark, New Jersey, where the letter had been brought up and claimed by both

Jesse R. Straughan

sides of the slavery controversy. When Lincoln heard that this church body claimed not to know where he stood on the matter he told the following story:

"That reminds me forcibly," he said, "of what occurred many years ago in Illinois. A farmer and his son were out in the woods one day hunting a sow. At length, after a long and fruitless search, they came to what they call a branch out there, where they found hog tracks and rootings-out for some distance on both sides of the branch. 'Now John,' said the old man, 'You take up on this side of the branch and I'll go up t'other, for I believe the old critter is on both sides'."

His friendship with Lincoln gave rise to an incident that was one of the favorite stories of his son, Henry M. Williams, father of Creighton Williams. On the occasion of a visit which Jesse L. Williams paid the President, a farmer had brought in an enormous watermelon as a gift. The President invited his guest to share the melon with him and the result was that the two powerful men consumed the entire melon.

"Who eats with me is my friend," said Lincoln. "And, watermelon is eating and drinking both."

Some interesting early history of Fort Wayne is given in a sketch of the First Presbyterian Church of Fort Wayne written by Jesse L. Williams and delivered by him on October 6, 1881, on the semi-centennial of its organization. It was his belief that few points in all the West furnished more promising material to the historian.

2

WHEN IN 1953 at the age af 100 years, Miss Caroline Straughan was carried upon a stretcher on board an air-liner headed for California where she was to live with two devoted nieces, she had just completed a cycle of immense proportions. The comfortable bed provided for her was in deference to her age. Her hands were encased in white gloves as was her custom when setting forth on a journey to church or a distant city.

For "Aunt Carrie" was the last surviving member of the family of Jesse Rittenhouse Straughan, chief engineer and superintendent of the Pittsburgh and Fort Wayne Railroad, forerunner of the Pennsylvania.

It was from the lips of Miss Caroline Straughan, Mt. Holyoke graduate, former teacher in the Clay and Hanna Schools of Fort Wayne, and the Chicago Schools for 20 years, that the history of the first railroad into Fort Wayne came to me in November, 1929.

It has been well over a century since the first Pennsylvania train made its entrance into Fort Wayne over shining rails. It was 3 o'clock in the morning, November 1, 1854, to be exact. And the little engine pulled in addition to the crew several prominent citizens and officials of the road.

The crew and passengers included Engineer Strope, Fireman James Davis, Conductor Pat Carr, J. R. Straughan, chief engineer and superintendent of the road; Judge Samuel Hanna, president, and Sam McElfatrick, resident engineer. They rode in on the engine from where Monroeville is today to this city.

Some of the newspaper clippings commemorating the event were in the possession of the Misses Jessie and Caroline Straughan, when they were still living in the Straughan residence, 321 E. Berry Street. They were the last surviving children of Jesse Rittenhouse Straughan who brought the Pennsylvania railroad to Fort Wayne. The residence was purchased by Mr. Straughan in 1854.

The story of Mr. Straughan takes us back to the days when a railroad was a strange and new device; when people had to be convinced of their need of such modern convenience; when money had to be raised; and when men of both means and vision were sufficiently scarce as to make the job of getting the bonds and money quite difficult.

Mr. Straughan was a civil engineer. He attended Hudson College, Cleveland, O., where manual training was combined with the classics. Cabinet-making was a required subject, and a boy was expected to turn out a certain amount of work with his hands. This young man had made a carved walnut bed and several fancy dressing glasses before he was 18, in addition to getting the groundword of his education in the classics. He also attended school at Cannonsburg, Pa., where he was expelled for a Halloween prank, and had to come home in disgrace to his Quaker father. For boys will be boys, you know, and there has never been an exception to that maxim.

These boys had committed considerable depredation, setting

fire to some outbuildings against which they had a grudge, and purloining some signs. They returned to their room to burn the signs in the Franklin stove. Came a knock on the door and one of the boys began praying in a loud voice. "A wicked and adulterous generation go about seeking a sign, but there shall be no sign given them," said the pious one. And the prayer continued until all the evidence was removed.

All of which goes to show Mr. Straughan's fitness for the job of empire-building. At least we know from that that he was a regular guy. And one who might be expected to walk every step of the way from Pittsburgh to Fort Wayne, laying out the Pennsylvania lines as he went. His achievement almost staggers one even in the light of modern progress.

For the old canal was considered by many quite adequate for all transportation purposes around Fort Wayne. What need was there of a railroad? You know the type. There would be no progress if we depended on their kind. The men responsible for Fort Wayne's progress had these objections to meet and overcome.

"Father was always on the road. Always traveling," Miss Caroline Straughan recalled. "He would go to New York, Boston, Philadelphia, whenever he would hear of a man with money who could be induced to help toward the building of the railroad. In these days it is not the job of the civil engineer to assume financial responsibility. But then there was no precedent to follow. Men had to do what had to be done."

And so step by step, rail by rail, the steel roadway was laid westward through Bucyrus, Crestline, Ft. Wayne and on to Chicago. They would lay the rails and then drive the engine on a little farther. Land would be bought and the right-of-way secured and the great steel artery would be extended.

Many was the fight over the right-of-way. Tom Swinney, who was a man of strong purpose, opposed the railroad with all his might. In fact, he went after Mr. Straughan with a shovel when he was approached about the right-of-way through his place, the land surrounding the Swinney Homestead. But even he could not block the plans. The railroad continued on its way and it made a fortune for Swinney.

"Many is the time mother had to cut his frozen boots and socks from his legs," Miss Straughan recalled.

"And many is the time he used to walk the distance from Bucyrus to Crestline," John M. Moderwell, an old friend of the family, recollected.

When the railroad reached Fort Wayne, Mr. Straughan decided to make his home here. He had a family of seven by this time and they had lived in towns all along the line. He was advised by William Rockhill to buy property in the west part of the city because all great cities grew toward the west. This was the way of the pioneer. Judge Hanna, on the other hand, advised him to settle in the east part of town. That was what he had done. It was a newer and more promising section, said Mr. Hanna.

Since the railroad had been extended through the city down Lafayette Street, Mr. Straughan decided to take Judge Hanna's advice. So he purchased the house at 321 East Berry Street, where his daughters lived at the time I interviewed them. He lived here for 51 years. The house had been built by Lawyer Cooper, the grandfather of Brown Cooper, as an office and residence. The original lock and great key were still in use in the front door.

"Gee what a key!", said the delivery boy who came there frequently.

The house had been left as it was built originally. All of the woodwork was black walnut disguised by graining to look like a lighter and cheaper wood. A fact that it is well to remember if the time should ever come when it is dismantled, as many of the old houses have been. (It has been dismantled, and I wonder what ever became of all that precious walnut woodwork?)

The impression I got from the story related by Miss Straughan was that the days of real romance were the early days. They were days of achievement such as we may never see again. There may be even greater achievements, building programs, skyscrapers, and expansion of every kind. But the pioneering days are over, at least in this country. That time is past. The foundation has been laid. And we can never quite know how much courage, strength of character, and vision were needed to bring railroads and highways across a wide continent.

"And all of the men of that day were not honest," Miss Straughan remarked. "Father had to meet many difficulties on account of unscrupulousness and ethics that he could not tolerate."

To go back to Mr. Straughan's young manhood: he was married to Miss Caroline Chambers of Marietta, O., a graduate of Dr. Cotton's Seminary for Young Ladies. The last word in female education in that day, it might be added. Those were great old days on the Ohio River, she used to tell her daughters.

"We had better times than you do now, I declare," she used to say.

They travelled by packet, for the Ohio River was the great highway to the West then. Miss Chambers had good times traveling back and forth from Zanesville to Marietta, and to Blennerhasset, an island in the Ohio. One of the gayest pictures in her memory was that of the young Mrs. Blennerhasset, an Irish lady, who brought some of her charming Old World customs to the new land. She wore a blue velvet riding habit with a graceful black hat and a sweeping white plume and she rode a white horse. For all the world like an Irish queen on a snow-white palfrey. She would be accompanied by a negro groom dressed in scarlet and the picture she made against the background of the forest, Mrs. Straughan could never forget.

Until a short time before, Miss Straughan told me, they had treasured one of the chairs from the old Blennerhasset home when it had been finally dismantled. The Blennerhasset's used to entertain lavishly all of the notables who came along these waterways. They had to leave the country on account of their connection with Aaron Burr in his fiasco.

As is usual even to the present day, the young engineers and surveyors created quite a stir among the feminine part of the population wherever they appeared. Mr. Straughan had started his career like George Washington with a surveying trip. He built the locks on the Muskingum, an Indian name meaning elk's eye. Here he became acquainted with young John Sherman, his rodman, and quite a beau at the time. John, the brother of General William T. Sherman, afterwards became quite a noted statesman. Mr. Straughan had entire charge of this engineering project, one of the most important undertakings of the time.

In 1848, when he was 30, he began to survey the Ohio and Pennsylvania Railroad. At the outbreak of the Civil War he was vice-president and chief engineer of the Spartanburg and Union Railroad of North and South Carolina. He had heard William Henry Harrison speak at Zanesville, O., in the campaign of 1840. He met Abraham Lincoln at Crestline, O., soon after Lincoln was elected president. He traveled with Stephen A. Douglas during the campaign of 1860 and heard Douglas address a political meeting at Columbus, S. C.

At one time he became very ill while engaged in work in the west. He was a passenger on the Union Pacific Railroad, and Will Combs, his rodman, took him off the train. In an old wagon which they were able to procure, they jolted along to Fort Gibson where they could receive medical assistance.

When the family came to Fort Wayne they stayed at the Hedekin House on Barr Street near Columbia, which was the "tony" hotel then. The building which later housed the Fort Wayne Mission was the first depot on the new road.

Mr. Straughan founded and named Crestline, O. He laid out the original town, after purchasing the 80 acres of land for $4,000. After he laid it out in town lots, he named it Crestline because it was on a crest of land. Later he disposed of three-fourths of the land, then gave it to the city fathers, and retained only one-fourth for himself. He is honored by this town as its founder.

The first American members of the Straughan family came to America in 1682, and Mr. Straughan's father laid out the south half of New Salem, O., in 1806. An indication of his perseverance is an incident related by one of his friends in a newspaper clipping. At one time he received a problem from this man. Seventeen years later during a momentary lull in his active career, he solved the problem. His death occurred in 1907 in his eighty-ninth year.

During World War I, the Misses Straughan received a letter of thanks from Franklin D. Roosevelt, assistant secretary of the navy, for the use of some of their father's binoculars, telescopes and spy-glasses as "eyes for the navy."

The trident and surveying instruments used by Mr. Straughan are in the Allen County-Fort Wayne Historical Museum. The pride cherished by the daughters of Mr. Straughan is due one who has made one of the outstanding contributions to the upbuilding of the Middle West.

Many rooms of handsome furniture and family heirlooms came out of that modest frame house. One of the items I am sure I had seen before. It was Mr. Straughan's special high-backed straight chair, fitted with springs on the front legs. I remember seeing the old man sitting in his chair on the stoop on sunny days, with a Lincolnsque shawl draped around his shoulders.

VI.
Grassroots to Skyline

1

"THERE IS A public building on the site of every residence I ever lived in as a child," Mrs. George Crane of 1203 West Jefferson Street told me one time. "And my birthday is celebrated all over the country," she added. "Every year I receive telegrams congratulating me on the occasion which is considered of prime importance to all loyal Americans.

Mrs. Crane was born on Abraham Lincoln's birthday. Among the buildings erected on the sites where she lived at various times are the Telephone Company, the Sheridan apartments, and the Jefferson School. Addie Edsall Crane remembered when Fort Wayne was just a village. She was born in 1845 in a house on East Main Street, diagonally across from the Court House — the frame building that replaced the first log Court House.

Addie Edsall, only daughter of John Edsall, was orphaned at the age of two. Her Aunt Jane and Uncle William Harvey Coombs took the little girl and reared her. And it could be said with all truth that she lived happily ever after. Although at times she admits she was "shifted about somewhat" among her relatives, she survived the shock of change and kept a bright cheery nature.

Her father was one of the nine children of Mrs. Peter Edsall who came to Fort Wayne in 1824 from Shane's Prairie (now Rockford, Ohio) after the death of her husband. The widow Edsall had conducted a boarding-house in a shanty at the site of the Greenville Treaty in 1814 and at the treaty at St. Mary's in 1817. These ventures had enabled her to purchase the family farm on Shane's Prairie (named for Anthony Chesne, French half-breed).

The five of the Edsall children to become identified with Fort Wayne and Allen County were Samuel, John, Simon, William S. Edsall, and Jane, who married Judge Coombs.

Although tragedy seemed to motivate many of the important events in Mrs. Crane's life, they never loaded her down with their weight. She had always been the center of a group of devoted relatives and friends. Birthdays, weddings, even funerals, have known her generous touch, as her collection of scrap-books testify.

Her scrap-books give a bird's-eye (may I say a Crane's?) view of Fort Wayne society over the years. The career of many a popular sub-deb and gallant World War veteran has been committed to the records of her scrap-books, which have been devoted to her favorites.

All of the significant occasions — historical, civic, social — which stirred the community during sixty years or more are included in these records; especially the weddings. It was on account of the weddings that I got in touch with her in 1929. By then she found it difficult to move about freely. But she was still full of effervescent charm. The paper boy laid her paper in her lap; the postman had orders to walk right in and help her with her voluminous mail if need be. (On her last birthday he even read the messages to her.)

For years she had been the champion baker of cakes for weddings and birthdays. Every size, style and form that these symbols could assume, Addie Crane was able to devise. Always she was much sought after for her cakes, and for the blessing that accompanied each one.

In her wedding-cake and special occasion industry, she was assisted by her daughter, Mrs. Frank Bond, who added the touches, comic and artistic, as the occasion demanded. If you remember the last time women wore their hair in a neat bun, you can see how both Mrs. Crane and Alice Crane Bond appeared in those days, and how Alice Bond still wears her hair today. Well, for a cake-baker, it was a most satisfactory style. No worry over hot tendrils of hair interferring with the creative part of their art, especially the boiled icing. For it was with boiling icing in a cornucopia that Mrs. Bond sculpted the unbelievable works of art they were called upon by some of their patrons to deliver. Which was the most difficult and original? Well, at least it was a "first!"

"What is his hobby?" asked Mrs. Bond when Mrs. James W. Dinnen asked her to perform her magic for a birthday cake for Dr. Dinnen.

"Well I'll tell you — it's his old sow and her brood. He

never talks about anything else, since he retired out here on the farm."

And so out of the pure white cornucopia came the pure white boiled icing to form his hobby — an old sow with her suckling pigs.

The birthday cakes as a rule had a giveaway date or year in the decorative heart. For Mrs. John Bass' birthday cake, she adroitly outlined a question-mark. When it came to Mr. Bass' birthdays, they offered a new challenge with every year. First it was a limousine, the first in town; then as the buffaloes were added and the fine cattle, the cake appeared with them immortalized in boiled icing on the top.

"'Nobody ever said 'no' to mother," her daughter recalls.

She was as adept at funerals as weddings and birthdays. Among her friends there were always those who needed her. When death came to these lonely people, it was Addie Crane who held the funeral at her house, if need be. When Sol D. Bayless died, an important figure in Masonic circles, she held the funeral in her home. In those days a home funeral included a meal for all the guests. There were 300 eggs boiled at that time, she remembered.

Her cake-baking skills were carried over to World War II, after her death, by Mrs. Bond who performed her most astounding decorating stunt. It was for a party given at Baer Field by the Service Men's Club for the members of the orchestra. Mrs. Bond took her late mother's largest cake-pan, the one she had used for the cake she baked for her uncle and aunt, Mr. and Mrs. William H. Coombs, on their 50th wedding anniversary. Around the edge of the huge cake she produced the figure of each man in the orchestra with his instrument. The drummer thought he was left out until the cake was turned around, and there he was with all his drums!

It was from her scrap-books on a fall day in 1929 that I had the privilege of copying some of the items that would have been lost if she had not saved them.

"Interesting reunion — Old and Young Settlers of Fort Wayne — They Meet at the Old Homestead of W. S. Edsall — Music, Light Grace and Beauty," read the headlines.

"The many friends of Mr. Edsall, during the last few days, have been in receipt of invitations for Wednesday evening,

THE GRANDMOTHER'S CLUB
AUGUST 7, 1914

Representative grandmothers of Fort Wayne 15 years ago are shown in this photograph of the Grandmothers' Club. Seated Center—Mrs. Anne Wilding (deceased) first president. Standing — Mrs. Brent Hartman, Mrs. Sarah Vesey (deceased), Mrs. George Crane, Mrs. D. L. Harding (deceased), Miss Emma Jenkinson (deceased), Mrs. Miles F. Porter, Mrs. Budd Van Sweringen, Mrs. Homer Hartman (deceased), Mrs. Stephen Morris. Mascot—George Crane Bond.

Mrs. "Ras" Chittenden, wife of town wit, author of "Ras Chittenden's Sea Diary."

April fifteenth, which indicated an intention to regenerate the old mansion by an elegant and fashionable SOIREE DANSANTE. About five hundred invitations were sent out, the majority of which met with a ready response and at 7 o'clock last evening, the full flood of light which streamed from every door and window in the house, and the natural sequence of carriages, the soft rush of encloaked ladies up the stairway, the gleam of dainty slippers, and billowy folds of tumultuous white dresses, on the way to the dressing-rooms, gave promise of the prolonged pleasure of the night. At half past 9 o'clock, the scene presented was a very brilliant one. The whole house was at the service of the glittering throngs of brave men and fair ladies. Music stole through the corridors and entranced the senses; music which, born of Johann Strauss, infused the feet to graceful motion and drew the visitors into the voluptuous mazes of the dance, floated in thrilling waves of sound out into the street and filled the air with melody.

"Under such circumstances, the enjoyment was keen and rapturous; the dressing was superb and poetic; the grace of Fort Wayne's fairest women gleamed within the brilliantly lighted parlors.

"The circumstances of the brilliant gathering were well-known and due honor and congratulations were tendered to the host, who was happiest among the happy. During the evening, and when the kaleidescopic changes in the brilliant salons were most attractive, Judge Lowry called the assembly to order."

An address embodying some of the pioneer history of Fort Wayne was read by Charles McCulloch. The guest list included the names of all the prominent people in the community, even to Mrs. Laura Suttenfield, who was referred to as the oldest settler in town. The Edsall house which was the scene of this party is still standing across Main Street from the former site of the Interurban Station.

No doubt the elegant affair was to honor Miss Jennie, only daughter of W. S. Edsall, before her marriage to Henry Colerick in 1871.

A brilliant tea at the "Pioneer Palace," the Swinney Homestead, was another of the social events recorded with verbal embellishments. It commemorated the golden anniversary of the building of the home. Mrs. Swinney was referred to by her maiden name, Lucy Taber, as one of the leaders of the "smart set," who lived in the old fort when the aboriginal settlers were in a vexed mood.

Among her choicest treasures is the Fort Wayne newspaper announcing Lincoln's death, with headlines in every variety of type filling a third of the column. All columns were marked by wide lines in black mourning with inverted rules.

A relic treasured by Mrs. Crane was a copy of Ras Chittenden's "Sea Diary," written by a fellow townsman, Erastus Ludlum Chittenden, member of the common council at the time of his second Atlantic voyage. The crossing from New York, July 10, 1875, on the Steamship Ville de Paris, took eleven days. He was also the town wag whose witticisms were current for many years.

"At 5 p.m. dinner was served. Many were called but few were chosen, the majority being laid up with sea sickness." His next door neighbor was sicker than seven large dogs and vowed to return over the land route.

Although much space is given to reviling the French for their vile language, he has nothing but praise for their cooking.

"I have just laid away very carefully a dish of fried frogs and many other comestibles beneath my vest. The dinner was simply grand, and although neither a gormand nor an epicure, I did enjoy it. Give me French cooking every time. No place in the world could furnish so great a variety of dishes, both foreign and domestic, as France. In Paris, if you strike the right cafes, as at Duval's, your sweet tooth, no matter how capricious, will be satisfied. The Chinese will find his 'swallow's nest' and rat pie, with chopsticks to eat it with, if desired. The Indian, his antelope, buffalo and golden corn. The turbaned Turk, his peculiar dishes, prepared according to the Mohammedan rites. The Jew, his orthodox preparations. The Russian his caviar and bear steak, while Johnny Crapo himself can revel in his fried frogs and claret. The Englishman can stuff his bay window full of his national dishes, roast beef and plum pudding, while the Yankee winks at him over his pumpkin pie and buck-wheat cakes, accompanied by his authentic sherry."

A very merry gentleman, forsooth, who comments on the open countenances of the sharks in the immediate wake of the vessel. "Like the whale they have no feathers," he remarks.

To a nearsighted lady on deck who observed him eating a banana and inquired if he were eating an orange, he replied, "No, a peanut," and she did not know the difference. Only her husband smiled.

Dissertations on sin, sickness, the immortality of the soul, fill many pages of the lively account which includes the solemn episode of a burial at sea.

Among the agreeable passengers he comments on a New York music teacher, "a plumptitudinous blonde who tears off excellent music. Who has been giving private lessons to Fifth and Madison Avenue ladies at $3 an hour."

As to Fort Wayne, no Chamber of Commerce enthusiast could be a better booster.

"In my travels during the year, to the Gulf on the South, to the Atlantic Coast on the East, through and among hundreds of growing towns and cities of our own continent, none show anywhere such substantial evidences of permanent growth, or vitality, enterprise and general prosperity as Fort Wayne, and I am proud to own her as my home, and register myself where 'ere I go as from the liveliest little city of her size to be found on the map. The bosom of her people would swell with conscious pride, could they have heard, as did I in New York, the compliments paid her on the gallant manner in which her banks, merchants and business men, generally, pulled through the devastating panic of September '73, that rocked the commercial world from center to circumference. While millionaires fell paupers, while once affluent bankers crawled forth in rags from the debris and ruins of their business, while mercantile houses tottered and fell throughout the land, Fort Wayne credit was unimpaired. The banks met their paper, merchants asked no discount on theirs, and the terrible commercial whirlwind passed harmlessly by. Toledo, Lafayette, Chicago and sister cities all about us, felt the shock, but Fort Wayne came out of the scorching ordeal unscathed, without a feather singed."

All this came out of Mrs. Crane's scrap-book.

The Edsall's who were associated with the Ewing's in the fur and pelt trade were among the first to make improvements on what is now West Main Street. W. S. Edsall, who gave the big party for his daughter, Jennie, before her marriage to Henry Colerick, was the grandfather of the late Guy Colerick and Mrs. Helen Colerick Achenbach.

As proof of her popularity, Mrs. Crane sited her old Domestic sewing machine, awarded to her in a contest for the most popular woman in Fort Wayne. All of the old bon vivants in town pushed that contest at the Princess Rink.

As we talked, the newsboy came into the room and laid the paper in her lap. "He always does this," she explained. "Someone has told him that it is hard for me to get to the door, so he has been instructed to put the paper where I can get it easily."

Life for Mrs. Crane was always like that.

2

There was nothing about the little lady in her black dress and white apron to indicate that a fugitive from the Guillotine, and a long-time fur-trader in the Indian country were the subjects of the stories she was to tell me that fall afternoon in 1929 when I talked with her among her photographs and clippings in a quiet parlor at 813 West Main Street.

Nevertheless, Mrs. Eudora Boyles, daughter of Lucien P. Ferry, pioneer attorney, and granddaughter of Louis Bourie, fur-trader and Indian interpreter, had quite a story locked inside of her. Some of it was what she remembered of the days when pilgrimages were made to her home to talk with her mother, Mrs. Caroline Bourie Ferry, up to her hundredth birthday in 1914 when she was photographed sitting in her favorite chair.

"Mother was the one who could tell the Indian tales. I never saw an Indian," she told me.

"Her father, Louis Bourie, came to this place from Detroit even before General Wayne came. Later they became warm personal friends. There were only two houses standing near the old English Fort between the St. Joseph and Maumee Rivers, in what was then known as the old Apple Orchard, now Lakeside. It was near these houses that grandfather built his house."

It is known that Louis Bourie traded extensively with the Indians first at Detroit, and later with the Pottawatomies at Coeur de Cerf, or Elkhart. From 1804 for six years he kept packhorses and a warehouse for the deposit and transportation of merchandise and peltries at the Maumee-Wabash Portage.

Mrs. Boyles' mother knew that her father had returned to Detroit, because that was where she was born in 1814.

"Mother was three months old in 1814 when they came back to Fort Wayne. She even thought she could remember that trip. But that was because when she was older they told her how they came by pirogue, a boat hewn from a large log, big enough to hold trunks, bedding, passengers, and a good stock of provisions for a long trip.

"When Grandfather Bourie arrived this time, he found his house burned to the ground. They said it had been fired by the Indians. However, it was learned that four or five log cabins near the fort that were used by him in trading had been burned by men of the garrison to prevent the Indians from burning them in a high wind during the siege of Fort Wayne in 1812.

"While the new house was being built on Columbia Street between Barr and Clinton, they lived in the fort and saw a great deal of the military life which was quite gay."

It is from Mrs. Boyles' mother, Mrs. Caroline Bourie Ferry, that we have the account of the pretty dresses of brocaded silks, satins and Canton crepes the ladies wore; the many parties for the officers and their families in the garrison. The men were resplendent in their military uniforms, while the civilians wore broadcloth suits with satin vests and ruffled shirts of linen and silk, with satin stocks.

This too might have been told Mrs. Ferry by her mother who was called "Lady Bourie" because of her refined ways and elegant dress as her portrait by Rockwell indicates. For the fort was evacuated when Caroline Bourie was only five years old.

After Louis Bourie's death in 1816, Caroline Bourie, her sisters and her mother went to live with a brother, John B. Bourie who had married and was living on East Columbia Street opposite their family home. She remembered also that in 1822 she was sent to school in the fort to the Baptist missionary Isaaac McCoy, along with ten English pupils, five French, eight Indians and one negro.

Next she went to school in the Council House which stood on East Main Street on the site of the Hedekin home, which then faced Columbia Street. The last school she attended was in the jail situated on the Court House square. Her recollection of the old well of the fort was that it was on the northwest corner where the Nickel Plate Railroad passes. One of the blockhouses stood close by the well.

In fact, what had happened in Mrs. Boyles' lifetime seemed pretty tame to her in comparison with the almost legendary life stories of her parents and grandparents that had been handed down in the family.

There was her grandfather, Pierre Peyre Ferri, Chef de Battalion to Napoleon the First, who found himself one day in the army of the doomed along with two friends, on the way to the Guillotine. As aristocrats, they had come under the condemnation of an order that glorified the Common Man in the name of Liberty, Equality and Fraternity. At one stop along the way near Paris, a peasant's cart stood close by them. As the story goes, nobody saw these three slip away. The next morning they rode into Paris disguised as a cartload of produce covered with a peasant's coat.

As Peter P. Ferry, one of the three refugees made his way to this country, to Monroe, Michigan, a settlement where there were many French. He had left a family behind him in France. Here he started life anew. He was the father of Lucien P. Ferry. A beautiful miniature of Mr. Ferry reveals the fine face of an aristrocrat.

"Mother could never forget how young father was when he died in August, 1844, — only 33 and so promising, too. She was a widow for 70 years," Mrs. Boyles recalled.

"Mother was only 17 and had returned home on vacation from school in Detroit when they met and were married. He was a promising young lawyer then at 21. There were no cookstoves, so she cooked their first meal in a fireplace ten feet long. In 1836 her husband bought a stove of some people travelling through Fort Wayne in a wagon, and folks used to come from miles around to see the curiosity."

Lucien P. Ferry was probate judge in Allen County for seven years, from October 5, 1836, to February 10, 1843. He had occasion to make many trips throughout the state. On one of these trips he accompanied Governor Samuel Bigger to Superior Court in Indianapolis. On the way they stopped for supper and overnight in a settler's home. As the woman of the house served their coffee, she asked which they preferred — long or short sweetening. Governor Bigger asked for "long." So she poured molasses into his cup. Mr. Ferry thought he would profit by his friend's experience and asked for "short." Whereupon his hostess bit a small piece of sugar from a lump and placed it in his cup.

The office and residence of Mr. Ferry were in the first block on Main Street west of Calhoun. It was here his children were born. Later he built a house next to the Rockhill House, which eventually became a part of St. Joseph's hospital, opposite the packet landing.

It was in September, 1843, that Mr. Ferry accompanied by Thomas Johnson another of the early lawyers, returned late one night from Bluffton, Wells County, where they had gone on Court business. They were overtaken by darkness and lost their way in a heavy downpour of rain that drenched them to the skin. Both men contracted a fatal illness on that trip.

The three Bourie girls all married prominent young men of early Fort Wayne. Harriet married Col. George Washington Ewing, and Nancy Ann married John P. Hedges.

"We used to travel on the packet to Monroe, Michigan, and other places on the line," Mrs. Boyles said. "That was a great experience. There was a band on the upper deck and when the packet arrived the band would play. Some packets carried produce. The boat was divided into rooms — kitchen, dining-room, and berths curtained off — and below there were stables for the horses. The boats were pulled usually by three horses.

"One time I tried to remember where I wanted to get off. We lived near the aqueduct, but I never could remember that word. So I nudged my friend, but she couldn't remember it either. So we had to come down to the foot of Broadway to the regular stop."

When Eudora Ferry was six years old she went to live with relatives in Monroe, Michigan. Later she attended the Young Ladies' Seminary at Albion, Michigan.

"When the boys in blue marched off to war they all passed our house on West Main Street on the way to Camp Allen. My sister Harriet was the prettiest girl in Fort Wayne and the boys used to wave and throw kisses to us as far as they could see us. I could see them nudge each other and pick out the prettiest.

"Then in 1861, Harriet married George Orvis. I remember the day Sumter fell and he brought the news to us at breakfast time. I can tell you we didn't eat any breakfast that morning."

Many of the memories of her mother, Mrs. Boyles kept in the booklet published by the Mary Penrose Wayne Chapter of the Daughters of the American Revolution.

There is one story that Mrs. Ferry's daughter did not tell. It happened in the year 1830 when the population of the town was not more than 200, with ten to 20 Indians to one white person. It is the story of Big Leg or Noweelinqua, a proud young Miami chief who was described by the white man as "a brave of impressive proportions, who never looked better than when mounted on a horse." He was also the best hunter of his tribe.

After several warnings, his discarded squaw continued to steal venison from his wigwam on the Indian reserve on the Wabash, eighteen miles from Fort Wayne. For this serious offense, Big Leg made up his mind to prove that his word was no idle boast. So he followed the offending squaw to Fort Wayne where she had sought refuge, and was employed in a tavern near the corner of Barr and Columbia Streets. Stalking his quarry with relentless cunning, as the story goes, he finally discovered her bending over a wash-tub in the yard of the tavern, and plunged his hunting-knife into her back.

Proud of his prowess and confident of approval as she fell dead at his feet, he even flourished the knife before the crowd of spectators who had gathered. But by this time the feeling of the community was such that a trial according to white man's justice was deemed necessary. It was decided to try the case of an Indian murder in a white man's court, for the first time, before Judge Charles H. Test, William N. Hood and L. G. Thompson. The Indian was put in jail where he was confined all summer. When the time for the trial rolled around, Bourie and Chief Richardville acted as interpreters. Two of the jurors — Jean Baptiste Godfroy and Henry Ossen — were also of Indian blood.

Of the family of Louis Bourie, only John B. Bourie, eldest son by an Indian mother of the Pottawatomies, was listed as "of Indian descent," in a treaty with the Pottawatomies, October 26, 1826, and had received a grant of one section of land on the Maumee adjoining the old boundary line of the military reservation. He was also a leading trader with an establishment on the northwest corner of Calhoun and Columbia Streets.

It is claimed that after a half-hour's deliberation, the jury handed down the verdict of "guilty" with a recommendation for mercy. Whereupon the judge pronounced the sentence, "To be hanged by the neck until he is dead, forty days hence."

Although Big Leg had heard the sentence pronounced, he could not understand what the words meant. This was a new thing to him. In all his experience as a hunter and warrior, he had never heard of such a penalty. Finally one of the lawyers suggested that the prisoner be asked if he had ever seen traders weigh with steelyards.

This he understood. To be weighed, he repeated. This made it clear to all the Indians. Accordingly word went through the tribe that Big Leg was to be weighed until he was dead. This news caused no little concern in his village. Big Leg was a good hunter. He killed most of the deer on which they lived. He was the most useful member of the tribe.

However, they could understand that the law must be fulfilled. For the shedding of blood, blood must be shed. So a council was named in Big Leg's village to devise a way for his redemption. Finally an expedient was hit upon that they believed would accomplish the purpose. In the village there was a lazy good-for-nothing Indian. The representatives of the plan came to town in a body to present their case to the jailer. They brought this Indian along. He was willing also to take the place of Big Leg.

All of this time Big Leg lay in jail waiting the day of his execution and contemplating the strange death he was to die. Bourie would send his sister Caroline, a girl of sixteen, to the jail with his meals. Into his tin cup she poured his coffee. Upon his tin plate she gave him portions of meat from the family table. One day he asked for his dog to be brought to him. It was done and he carried out an experiment in his own way. He "tried it on the dog." Then he handed down his decision. "I weigh dog. Him very sick. Shoot, stab, tomahawk me Indian way. White man's way no good."

When the impropriety of inflicting capital punishment upon this ignorant Indian was apparent to all, the case was presented to David Wallace, special prosecutor at the 1828 terms of the Circuit Court at Fort Wayne, and a member of the Indiana legislature. Young Wallace evidently deemed it humane to grant executive pardon to this ward of our government who had honestly proved his ignorance of the law. Thus was Big Leg reprieved from his threatened execution and returned to his village on the Wabash to resume his vocation as a hunter.

In 1846 the last of the Miamis were finally gathered together for the final journey on canalboats which passed through Fort Wayne on their way by canal and river to the Ohio. As the canal boats loosed their moorings, many of the bystanders were moved to tears at the sight of their sober saddened faces. The final removal of the tribe was reported in local papers on October 20, 1846.

Caroline Bourie Ferry, a young widow, was among those who watched this pitiful group.

"I remember this Indian distinctly," the late Bert J. Griswold quotes Mrs. Ferry as saying. "While he was confined in the log jail in the court house square I took his food to him. He would reach out through the bars of the window with his tin cup, and into this I poured his coffee. I was a girl of seventeen. When the members of his tribe were taken to the west this man went with them. I remember the scene very well — how many of them were bound by the hands with ropes. The younger ones were willing to go, but the older men and women fought against leaving their old homes. This man, as he looked around at the crowd, saw me and recognized me as the girl who had been bringing his food. He came and thanked me for what he thought was my great kindness."

This was the last ever seen in these parts of the Miami Chief Noweelinqua or Big Leg, as he was called by his friend the white man.

Although Lucien P. Ferry died so early in life, he left an honorable name even as far west as the state of Washington. His brother, Elisha P. Ferry became the first governor of that state after serving eight years as territorial governor under Lincoln. He and Lincoln were close friends, had studied law together in Illinois.

The Fort Wayne papers used to carry such items as "Col. C. P. Ferry, the Duke of Tacoma, visits here." This was the son of Lucien P. Ferry, an elder brother of Mrs. Boyles. He had gone west, bought land in Tacoma in 1868, and gained the title "Duke" when Tacoma land was worthless. But his vision and judgment proved to be good and he became one of the richest men in the West. The great Washington State Historical Society and Ferry Museum bears his name and is a monument to his philanthropies. He became Consul to France, and during World War I, his grandchildren fought in both the allied and the German armies. A daughter who married a German continued to live in Stuttgart.

"My father's favorite hymn was 'A Charge To Keep Have I.' I remember when the first Episcopal Church was being built on the corner of Berry and Harrison, and services were held in the Court House. My father and Peter P. Bailey would alternate in leading the service. Mr. Bailey would always choose the hymn, 'I Would Not Live Always.'

"And this is my favorite text," Mrs. Boyles said as she handed me Isaiah 30:21. "And thine ears shall hear a word behind thee saying, 'this is the way, walk ye in it, when ye turn to the right hand, and when ye turn to the left'. It has helped me always and I will pass it on to you."

The granddaughter of a French "aristocrat" and a French fur trader had told me what was uppermost in her mind of her family history.

VII.
The Tale of the Shirtwaist

1

THIS IS THE TALE of the shirtwaist, that neat tailored item of bought by women. Women were wearing boys' plain shirts for eighties and continued its popularity for three decades. If you recall the leg-o'mutton sleeve, the pannier, the tight basque, the dolman and the polonaise, of the preceding decade or so, you will not wonder at the shirtwaist. It was time someone came to the rescue of women and emancipated them from the slavery of their dress.

About 1885 the great emancipator was at hand. Little did he think that the straw he grasped in order to save him and his business from utter ruin would prove to be so strong and durable. He was in fact Samuel M. Foster, the inventor of the ladies' shirtwaist.

Like many important discoveries, this one had a very small beginning. A steaming tea kettle, a key on a kite, had the power to set a fertile brain to work on mighty problems. A faded rag of a boy's waist started the ladies shirtwaist. This is how it all happened.

Samuel M. Foster was proprietor of a small dry goods business on Calhoun Street in the early eighties. He had graduated from Yale University at the age of 27, had taken a fling at journalism by publishing the Dayton Daily Herald, and had started a small dry goods business at Danville, Ill. He was at last engaged in a third commercial venture, which appeared to be a failing dry goods business in Fort Wayne.

But the resourceful man knows when it is necessary to administer artificial respiration, to breathe new life into an expiring business. Sam Foster recognized the signs of rapidly approaching death to his venture. He determined to do something about it.

During the winter of 1884-85 things were looking their very worst. The year before they had sold a boy's waist for a low price and it had gone very well. The thought came to the proprietor that they might try to manufacture these waists as a last resort. Not one sample of the last year's stock was to be had in the store, however. So one of the clerks brought from home a faded little blouse that his small boy had worn for many months. With his own hands, Mr. Foster ripped the garment apart and laid it down on paper as a pattern. With this as a model he started his idle clerks to cutting boys' waists out of cheap material. A small factory was started right in the store. The original garment had sold for 19 cents. The new one of better material sold for a little more.

With this as a humble start, the business grew moderately, and salesmen sold the garments over a short circuit of surrounding towns. Now no detail is too important for the little struggling business to learn from. It appeared after a year or more that 14 was the most popular size. Why was that? Mr. Foster wondered and followed up with some inquiries. He found out why.

The salesmen reported that these larger sizes were being bought by women. Women wearing boys' plain shirts for tennis! Well, that was an idea! Mr. Foster set to work. He cut out more fourteens than any other size. His salesmen had a new idea for the market. It was called a ladies' shirtwaist. It came in a variety of materials and figures: fine stripes, polka dots, and in black and white and colors.

"It took two years for the idea to take hold," Mr. Foster told me. "Then it became the rage all over the country. As far as I know, I was the pioneer manufacturer of the ladies' shirtwaist. And such a vogue as it had! Do you know of any other item of feminine apparel that continued to be popular for 39 years?"

The rise and fall of the shirtwaist marked a transistion period in women's dress. It ushered in the tailored garment for women, which is especially becoming to certain types. The first real tailored girl was the shirtwaist girl. The garment continued to hold its sway in varying forms through the era of the Gibson girl, the bicycle age, the fudge-making period of the early century and on up to the day of the one-piece dress.

With the close of the World War it became clear that the shirtwaist had had its day. Then the Foster Shirtwaist factory, which had supplied the insistent demand for 30 years, modified its business to meet the new demand. The shirtwaist had grown up to be a dress, and the manufacturer continued to make women's garments.

The first shirtwaists were exact duplicates of the boys' shirt. Then slight variations began to appear. They had stiff separate collars with tailored ties, stiff cuffs with links. The separate waist called for the separate skirt, the jacket suit and the separate belt. In this latter detail the love of adornment, which in the human race is usually confined to the feminine sex, made its appearance. Fancy buckles, jewelled and elaborate, furnished the only luxurious touch to the austere costume. Shirtwaist sets consisting of studs and links appeared in a variety of feminine versions.

As time went on, the shirtwaist was adapted to many variations. It was made of French flannel, silk, sheer handkerchief linen and other materials. It appeared with trimming of Irish crochet, Mexican drawnwork, Philippine embroidery. It came from the ends of the earth with a new character in each of its manifestations.

Nimble brown fingers plied the loom in the manufacture of Philippine grasscloth patterns to be used in American shirtwaists. Japanese and Chinese fabrics were embroidered and used for a sort of glorified shirtwaist. Women travellers all over the world wore the American shirtwaist on shipboard and train. The pyramids of Egypt, the Taj Mahal of India, the ruins of Greece and Rome were gazed upon by armies of women wearing the familiar shirtwaist in all its varied forms. It was peculiarly suitable for traveling and its use was almost universal.

At first the accepted style always had a yoke in the back and was neatly belted at the waistline. The mannish collar gave way in time to the more feminine turnover collar with a ribbon bow. The shirtwaist girl was just as dainty and feminine in her day as the more elaborately adorned generations which followed and preceded her.

Moreover it simplified many things.

It was not necessary for the mothers of that day to pass resolutions and establish laws to curb the desire for too fine plumage among the high school girls. No matter how much money one had to spend on clothes, the high school girl who looked her best wore a shirtwaist and skirt. Possibly her skirt was lined with silk in deference to a taste for luxury, and was worn over silk petticoats. Yes, several of them! But the general effect was the same. The silk underlinings only tended to give a more musical swish, swish. It just sounded more elegant. Few girls required silk, however.

Miss Alice Stocking who had been a clerk in the store when Sam Foster got his "shirtwaist" inspiration, continued as forelady in the Foster Shirtwaist Factory for twenty-five years.

S. M. Foster
as a college boy in 1879.

Tennis club on court at 47 East Lewis Street, 1889. Left to right, Bessie Baldwin, Hal Joss, Connie Lumbard, ..., Nebe Baldwin, Alice Ward, Georgia Lumbard, Nellie Caswell, ..., Dave Randall.

THE TALE OF THE SHIRTWAIST

Do you remember the original Gibson girl? And pray what did this paragon of feminine beauty wear? A shirtwaist and skirt. She was slender of waist and had a graceful curve from shoulder to hip and thence down to the hem of her ankle length skirt. And was she beautiful? Ask the college boys of yesteryear. Her picture was as much a fixture on dormitory walls as the pin-ups of today.

In fact the shirtwaist girl survived many a frivolous mode. Note, for instance the Merry Widow hat, the most absurd of the variations of the sailor hat. She lived to see the overthrow of the hatpin and the downfall of the plural underskirt. Modern chiffon apparel would have looked pretty clumsy to her. A certain clean-cut grooming was lost when she passed. And certain new words such as allure, glamor, charm and subtlety came into the bright lexicon of the designer.

The shirtwaist girl never heard of sex appeal. And yet there are those who can testify to the fact that she had "IT" no less than the most modern woman.

The little struggling business that had been about to die on its feet when Mr. Foster got his shirtwaist inspiration soon outgrew its limited quarters in the store. When the idea of the garment had taken a firm enough hold on the women of the country, the Foster Shirtwaist Factory was established on East Columbia Street.

The Foster Shirtwaist Factory flourished in its Columbia Street location for many years. The pattern that Mr. Foster had haggled out with a jack-knife, he admits should have been framed and preserved as a museum piece. At the moment it seemed like a queer occupation for a Yale graduate. But only time could prove what energy and resourcefulness could do in a case like this.

Moreover the business offered agreeable work to hundreds of women and girls. Women just naturally knew how to cut, fit and sew. It was one of the important industrial opportunities offered to the women in Fort Wayne.

Unlike the song of the shirt, the romance of the shirtwaist was not founded on human suffering. It employed no child labor. It offered pleasant working conditions throughout its history. As I talked with Mr. Foster, it numbered among its employes some who had been with the business since its very earliest beginning. Miss Alice Stocking, to name one, who held her place as forewoman for 25 years, had been a clerk in the store when Mr. Foster got his inspiration. It was a business that belongs distinctly to Fort Wayne and marked a new industrial epoch in our business life.

It has been only one of the many interests of Mr. Foster, whose connections both commercial and civic were legion. But it was the activity that expressed the energy and resourcefulness of its originator more than anything else he has ever done. Samuel M. Foster, the inventor of the ladies' shirtwaist! The fact should go down in the history of the community as one of the outstanding achievements of its day. Let Paris have her couturieres and her Rue de la Paix! Fort Wayne was the birthplace and home of the American ladies' shirtwaist!

2

Young ladies who walked down West Berry Street in 1864 were not surprised to find themselves escorted by a fat, grunting porker. Little children of the seventies on their way to kindergarten in the fashionable West End were sometimes frightened by a flock of geese with heads held as high as their own.

The first time Miss Adeline Wells, daughter of Dr. Arnold Wells, Fort Wayne's pioneer dentist, took a walk down Berry Street she was forced to follow a pig.

"The pig met me at Maiden Lane and I tried to poke him into the gutter. But he grunted on undismayed by my efforts to get rid of my escort. Finally "Em" Woodworth, who was a 'card', gave him such a shove that he had to abandon his plan to walk on the sidewalk in front of two young ladies and take to the street instead."

Mrs. W. E. Griffiths, when living at 1011 Oakdale Drive, who came to Fort Wayne as Adeline Wells in 1864, remembered a great deal about her family as well as the expressions of mob feeling during the Civil War and post Civil War years.

The first time her daughter May went to kindergarten, she felt secure in the grasp of her mother's hand. The next day she met the flock of geese and was frightened out of her wits so that she returned home in tears and refused to go on with her education that day.

"We came, in 1864, from Akron on the railroad, I recall," said Mrs. Griffiths. "And we stayed at the Rockhill Tavern, which faced the canal. The first party I attended after we came here was at the Rockhill house which has been torn down recently, where it stood as a part of the old building of St. Joseph's Hospital."

Dr. Wells and his family lived in the frame house which stood where the Chamber of Commerce stood later. His office was at the corner of Berry and Calhoun Streets in a brick building with a wrought iron railing on the outside. It stood where the Old National Bank was in 1930. Dr. Wells was a contemporary of Dr. Isaac Knapp and was a very skillful craftsman in his field. He was the inventor of porcelain teeth and of a seamless porcelain plate. He worked by a process that was original and which nobody else seemed able to learn.

"When he carved the teeth he sat on a high stool before a shelf which crossed the center of an uncurtained window. On the shelf before him was a plaster cast of the human jaw, on which rested the plate of finer texture which he was carving. He had no model and using a small penknife carved from memory, swiftly, perfectly, a set of teeth adapted to the face of the wearer. Dr. Wells could never teach anyone to do the carving, but when his health began to fail he taught a local dentist to mend broken plates perfectly. Judge Coombs and his wife and others had duplicate plates made before Dr. Wells' failing health compelled him to give up his practice," wrote Mrs. Griffiths in a life of her father.

His work was exhibited in Philadelphia and other eastern cities. Dr. Wells must have been quite a character in his time. His coming to Fort Wayne was singular to begin with. He was a Democrat, a war Democrat. He agreed with Mr. Lincoln on the proposal to reimburse the South in money for their slaves. He believed in the war also, and had two sons in the conflict.

Anyone who has ever lived through any war period can realize the hatreds and prejudices, the mob feeling that is engendered by differences of opinion. Men are robbed of all reason, of all tolerance and brotherly love in the issues of the moment. There are no political bitterness as great as that of the Civil War, Mrs. Griffiths believed.

[85]

"I know what an angry mob is like," said Mrs. Griffiths. "And I shall never forget the abject terror I felt when as a schoolgirl I witnessed a mob in action in Akron. A poor woman was pacing the banks of the canal, wringing her hands and shrieking. A man was on the end of a rope being dragged up and down the canal. We thought the rope was around his neck, but we found out that it was under his arms, so that he emerged only exhausted and spent from his ducking in icy water in midwinter."

The man was a friend of her father's, a Democrat, and feeling was high. Akron was the end of the underground railway and strong abolition territory. Her father finally went to Louisville, intending to have his family follow. But the war broke out in the meantime and he did not want to bring his family to a border state. He had enjoyed living in the south and on his return he continued to express his opinion to his own undoing.

"Many Democrats were mobbed in Akron that year and his turn was to come. In a lonely spot where the West Main Street bridge crosses the canal he was knocked down and beaten and his jaw dislocated. He set his own jaw bone and finally reached his west hill home. Some necessary clothing was packed in a small satchel. He walked to a nearby town, purchased a horse and buggy and drove to Cleveland."

The climate of the lake city proved too rigorous for him and in looking for an inland city he selected Fort Wayne. There was only one Negro family here at the time, strongly Democratic in its sentiment. He had been carrying gold in a belt around his waist for some time, as he realized his would be the fate of all Democrats in that Ohio vicinity.

The story of his life is just as romantic in some of the earlier chapters. He was born in Danville, Vermont, in 1805, going from there at an early age to New York City, where he became a fitter of fine boots and shoes and married Maria Van Kuren, of Dutch descent.

Mrs. Griffiths recalled seeing her mother hold a candle in one hand as she sat steady and calm while her husband pulled her teeth. In these days when life is made safe for nerves by gas and other humane devices, it seems like heroic courage.

They started west intending to go to Chicago, stopping on the way to visit a cousin, who was a lawyer in Coshocton, Ohio. Here they stopped and Wells studied law and was admitted to the bar. He became a law partner of his cousin and continued practicing for several years until his cousin's death. They proceeded westward once more, stopping in Akron, where several of their friends from the east had settled. Suddenly the canal froze over and they were obliged to stay until spring. Before the canal opened, Wells had established himself in a good shoe business, which encouraged him to remain there for many years.

He had a restless mind and never tired of studying. All that he could accumulate of property and money was of value to him only as it enabled him to pursue his work and his study. He sold his shoe business and studied medicine finally, securing a diploma and practicing for several years. But his health made it impossible for him to continue with the strenuous practice that the early doctor had to have in the days before telephone and automobile. And it was then that he took up the dentistry, which he followed so successfully to the end of his life.

Mrs. Griffiths recalled her girlhood home in Akron which the family left regretfully to come to Fort Wayne.

"When we arrived my mother sat down on the steps of the frame house my father had bought for us here and cried for her beautiful home back in Ohio.

"We used candles all over the house in this old home. And mother did all of the sewing for the family by hand, even the fine stocks and shirts for the menfolks. The children used to sit around a big table in the living room while our parents read Bacon, Shakespeare, Voltaire and the Bible aloud. There were seven depressions in the hearth where the seven children cracked their nuts.

"The porcelain plates for the dental work were baked several times in a furnace. There was a large abandoned fireplace in the first home we had in Akron, and Dr. Wells had his furnace built in the fireplace. The first time it was fired it burned the house to the ground. I went with him the next morning to view the ground. The furnace and its contents were all right. The chimney and the Dutch over were perfect and the family cat sat in its accustomed corner of the hearth placidly washing its face. Before cold weather came, a substantial brick residence stood on the same ground with the furnace in a shed in the garden."

Finds Many Friends

In Fort Wayne they found many congenial friends who had come from the East. There was not a two-story house in the block on West Wayne Street where their home stood. The old Methodist College stood at the end of Wayne Street. And many were the pranks played by the students of that day.

One night she recalls that a professor was putting his buggy up in the barn when he heard students whispering outside. Expecting mischief he slipped into the buggy seat and drew the storm apron to conceal himself. The barn door opened and four students, two to push and two to pull, ran the buggy across the road and back of the college where the ground sloped to a shallow ford. They found it easy to run the buggy down hill to the middle of the river. Here the professor appeared and told them he had enjoyed the ride, but they would have to take him back or he would report them in the morning. It proved a hard pull up the hill and out of clay mud.

In those days it was possible to circulate legends about ghosts and create not a little excitement. Images of the Goddess of Liberty projected from the dissecting room of the institution presumably by students created a very spooky effect with the aid of mist arising from the river.

Mrs. Griffiths studied trigonometry and Latin in a class with several of the men students which included Gif Lowry and Willis Case, the son of a Senator. She also knew James H. Smart when he was superintendent of the Fort Wayne schools.

As president of the Woman's Club league from 1904 to 1906, Mrs. Griffiths had the honor of assisting at the birth of many substantial movements for the welfare of the community. The building of the Public Library was due largely to the efforts of the women of the league in securing the Carnegie donation and the local fund necessary for the building.

Donation to Art School

At the first meeting of the league in the library building, a donation of $250 was given to the art school and a civic department was added to the league. An arts and crafts association was also formed and a fine exhibit of hand-made jewelry and rugs was brought from the east just before Christmas and displayed with local articles at the art school which was in the building still standing at the corner of Wayne and Webster Streets.

The league also offered to pay the salary of a teacher of domestic science if the school board would provide a room in the new Central High School Building. Under this arrangement, lessons in cutting, fitting, sewing and cooking were given to the students under the sponsorship of the domestic science department of the league of which Mrs. O. N. Guldlin was the chairman.

At this time, also Miss Catherine Hamilton offered the use of a vacant lot near the high school for the first playground which was thus located in the section where it was needed most. Many children lived above stores and had no suitable place for play. This was accomplished by the educational departments of the club of which Mrs. J. N. Study was the chairman.

Fort Wayne's reputation as the "Garden City" was achieved, Mrs. Griffiths pointed out, during these years when the club league instituted the distribution of seeds to the school children. The first flower show was held in the old high school building on East Wayne Street and prizes of garden tools and tulip and daffodil bulbs distributed.

The women who labored to fill the seed packets the first year took especial pride in the beautifully kept lawns and attractive gardens which are to be found now in all parts of the city. Theirs were the pioneer efforts in this work. And many of them got what Mrs. Griffiths designates as the "alley eye" and could not enjoy a walk on any of the city's streets without glancing up the length of the alleys to see if they had been cleaned according to the city ordinance.

"Except serving four years on the book committee of the Public Library, this is the only service I have ever given to our city," she stated, adding in parenthesis, "I rocked the cradle twenty years."

VIII.
Saloons vs. Short Skirts

1

When saloons went out, short skirts came in. And simultaneously the emphasis was changed from wine to women. The danger of this country today is from licentiousness, which has always been the greatest danger in the world.

This was the observation of Judge Samuel M. Hench, oldest lawyer of the Allen County Bar, and the only Civil War soldier-lawyer in northern Indiana, it is believed.

As soldier, politician, student of history, able lawyer, judge, Judge Hench devoted long years to observation and study of the important problems before the world.

The first great problem to engage his attention was slavery. He fought in the war of the Rebellion, and bore grave wounds as a result of his part in the conflict.

"Whenever a law strikes at a man's property, it causes hatred and dissension that it takes generations to overcome and forget. This was true of slavery. It is also true of prohibition. Two years were not long enough to give dealers to dispose of their liquor. Vast sums of money had been tied up in property for the conduct of a business that was perfectly legal up to the passage of the eighteenth amendment.

"Fifteen years should have been allowed for prohibition to take effect. In that time it would have been accomplished effectively. And there would have been no cause for the excessive bitterness on the part of those who held valuable property used in carrying on the traffic. The change was too sudden. The country was bound to suffer. Readjustment could not be made so quickly."

In his comments on important personages of his time, he never failed to point out those who were incapacitated because of their intemperance.

"They exercised their arms too much", he commented in speaking of the men who were continually engaged in carrying the cup to the lip. This country was in a bad way morally, he believed. And he shook his head gravely. "This is a light-minded generation," he insisted. There are symptoms of decay. Other nations have risen to the heights and have fallen. And the cause has been ever the same."

Like a hoary prophet beseeching his people to repent and turn again to the ways of righteousness, Judge Hench pointed to other great nations that have gone down to oblivion. Ninevah, Babylon, Susa, Tyre, Sidon. Rome and Jerusalem had their downfall. And the cause was licentiousness, he believed.

"Paris has been the Babylon of the world for 200 years. As long as we let her dictate our fashions and our morals we are in danger of the greatest of all evils. This is a lax generation. And it shows just as it has in other great civilizations. It can be seen especially in the dress and morals."

Curiously enough, the extremes and absurdities in dress, especially in women's dress, came in with prohibition, he pointed out, thus giving the student of morals reason to believe that there was something in the nature of cause and effect in the phenomenon.

Wine, women and song have held together as the slogan of the desolute and merry gentlement of every age. Take away the wine and what have you?

There may be something in it.

For after all, the prophets and sages have been men of maturity and wisdom. There is something that comes with long years of contemplation. And sometimes when a man is removed from the busy marts of trade and commerce, he can arrive at truths that do not come otherwise.

Not that Judge Hench could be called a hermit. He lived in the midst of life. His rooms at the corner of Main and Clinton Streets were but a stone's throw from the Court House which had been the arena of his combats for so many years. But he was a wise and thoughtful man, a curious survival of a slower, statelier age. And he viewed the current scene with eyes that saw through and beyond its apparently meaningless clatter.

Nor did he go about preaching an approaching doom. When he could be caught at rare times in reminiscent mood, he gave utterance to bits of wisdom, history, world affairs, observations, deductions, and memories of both men and events.

The gleam of the coal fire in the old-fashioned base-burner

in his rooms would flare up and seem to bring back the memories.

When I called on him, Judge Hench's stove had kept him warm for 33 winters. It was better than a furnace. He could sit in silent thought, reach out his hand and change the drafts without moving from his chair. Life was very simple and comfortable as it should be for an aging philosopher. He should not be bothered with too many material things.

"Yes, I came to Fort Wayne in August, 1863," he ruminated. "And I carried my carpet-bag in my hand as I walked down Calhoun Street at 6 o'clock in the morning. I had left my small trunk at the station. It is in the back room as good as new. It cost $4.50 when I bought is back home in Pennsylvania.

"Where was I born? Why I was born a respectable distance from the foot of the Tuscarora Mountains in Juniata County, Pennsylvania, in 1846. Now where was I when you asked me that question? Oh, yes, the Battle of Fredericksburg. That was December 13, 1862. I walked off the field to the base hospital. My gun was smashed in my hands, and my right ear was all but torn away. My hearing has never been the same. And I had many other wounds.

"I remember we marched right around the grave of Mary Washington, the mother of George Washington."

This was the tall venturesome youth who left home to join the troops and was seriously wounded by Confederate shells early in the war. But he walked off the field in spite of his wounds and came to the division hospital near the city of Fredericksburg. It was as clear in his mind as if it had happened yesterday. Years of legal practice had given to a naturally fine mind a precision and accuracy that time had not lessened.

Men, places and events, causes and effects were all there. Sometimes it took a bit of studying to bring it all into the proper focus. But there were no mistakes about it. This youthful soldier came then to Fort Wayne. But the call to arms was too much for him. While on a visit with relatives in Peoria, Ill., he re-enlisted in Company R, One Hundred Thirty-ninth Illinois Infantry. The troops went by boat down the river to Paducah, Ky., and were on the battle line within twenty-eight hours.

When the four months service was up he returned to Fort Wayne and later enlisted in Company 3, One Hundred Eighty-third Indiana regiment. His youth and wounds would have made it impossible for him to be accepted in a regiment near home. Like all youth, when the call comes, it is the most glorious call that youth ever hears until the first shell passes overhead, he added.

"People ask me how I could fight in the War of the Rebellion and then vote the Democratic ticket all my life. And I tell them that I was in favor of the Union of Washington, Jefferson, Monroe, John Adams and Patrick Henry. I was fighting to preserve the Union."

Democrat or not, however, the greatest man in Indiana at that time was in the Republican party—Senator James E. Watson. For the Judge has ever had an eye for picturesque personalities. He belongs to the day when people expressed themselves in no uncertain terms, when oratory was real oratory. Moreover, he had a chance to know and admire most of the prominent men of his day.

"And for every great man there is a great unusual mother. Did you ever notice that?" he inquired earnestly.

"It is something I have always observed and made a study of. Take Jonathon Edwards, the grandfather of Aaron Burr, Jeremiah S. Black, Alexander Campbell, Matt Carpenter, James A. Garfield and John G. Carlyle, to name only a few of the great men I have known most about. They all had great mothers.

"A man has to be big from the neck up. A big man shows it in his head and face. Take Henry Colerick, for instance. They called him the "Little Giant". And when we went into a hotel lobby together as we used to do years ago, all necks were craned to see who he was. He was a fine-looking man.

"And Bryan at the height of his powers was the finest-looking man I ever saw. 'The front of Jove himself . . . and eyes like Mars to threaten and command.' With a beautiful head of black hair."

Bryan had made a triumphal entry into Fort Wayne in June, 1895, Judge Hench recalled. He spoke before a mass-meeting at the Sanger-bund Hall which stood at the corner of Main Street and Maiden Lane. Judge Hench assisted in the arrangements for the important event. He owned horses and used to be an impressive figure in all local parades, his friends recall. On this occasion he drove with Bryan all over Fort Wayne as he showed him the spots of interest.

The speaker was introduced by Judge Robert Lowry, and the speech was enthusiastically received. It was a great occasion. And after all is said and done, he believed that Bryan was the individual who did more to bring about the passage of the Eighteenth Amendment than anyone else.

"If there ever was a Christian statesman, Bryan was one," he said.

He recalled many of the picturesque characters about the town. There was the Hon. Ras Chittenden, a great character and no bigger than a 10-cent cigar; but as keen and clever as a man could be. His wise-cracks have come down to this day.

"Of course I don't really believe that one church is any better than another. But I am a Presbyterian, and there is something about the Presbyterian Church that goes with a clean shirt, education and minding your own business", said the Judge as he picked up a Presbyterian hymnal from among the pile of books in a small book case.

His favorite hymn, by the way, was "Abide With Me."

Books were then and had been always his nearest companions. His rooms were lined with them. His was probably one of the best law libraries outside of Indianapolis, with an especially complete collection of books on criminal law and a very large number on civil law.

His grandparents on his mother's side came from Ireland to this country in 1787 when General Washington was presiding over the Constitutional Convention. His first American ancestor came to Chester County, Pennsylvania, from Saxony in 1732.

Judge Hench was probably the only man left in Fort Wayne who wound his watch with a key. He was carrying the same watch he had purchased of J. Ferdinand Pietz in 1878. It cost $90 including the chain and key. The stem-wind device had just come into use, the jeweler explained, but it cost an additional $35. So he purchased the handsome gold watch which he still carried, and he wound it up nightly with a key carried on the chain.

SALOONS VS. SHORT SKIRTS

In spite of his fine old courtliness, or possibly because of it, Judge Hench had his doubts about women's Suffrage. He had very serious doubts. Just exactly what they were I am not able to state. But it had something to do with his belief that so far nothing epochal had been accomplished by women's entrance into the political arena.

"The first great cause least understood", he quoted from Alexander Pope's Universal Prayer, in reference to his religious convictions. Having read Tom Paine and Darwin as a young man and thoroughly digested and disposed of them, he had a faith that had withstood the test of time.

His recipe for happiness was something like this: Follow the Golden Rule, never bet on the other fellow's game, and vote the Democratic ticket.

Judge Hench held many important offices in the county and state during his many years of active practice. He was judge of the criminal and the superior courts of Allen County, and a past department prosecuting attorney from 1874 to 1881, and was a member of the Indiana legislature in the house of representatives in 1891 and 1893. He was also a member of the managing board of the Soldiers and Sailors Monument at Indianapolis for eight years, and had charge of the law division of the comptroller's office of the Treasury Department under Cleveland's administration in 1888.

There is just one thing about Judge Hench that remains unexplained. And no amount of explaining will do any good at this late day. Was he the judge who rode away that summer's day so long ago with only the empty memory of what might have been?

I doubt if we shall ever know. For he belongs to the generation of those who may ride away, but on the other hand, never tell.

2

Every proper story should have a heroine as everybody knows. Whatever our views on women may be in private life, we just can't get along without them in history and literature. So this story has a heroine . . . A heroine who was the inspiration in the lives of a number of men . . . A heroine who gave them Godspeed on their careers, who encouraged them when they were weak, and rejoiced with them when they were strong and successful. In short, our heroine is Harriet Scott Foster, the energetic mother of six sons, two of whom were David N. and Samuel M. Foster of this city.

"We got our drive and energy from our mother, I believe", said D. N. Foster in a conversation with me in the office of the park board in 1930. He realized how important is the kind of mothers men have.

"Do you realize that not one of the founders of this nation, with the exception of the Adams family, was the founder of a distinguished family?" he said. "And do you know why that is?", he said.

To which I contributed my own theory that possibly the prettiest brides did not always make the best ancestors. And we agreed that the founding fathers either did not realize that or did not care, because some of them seemed to have married the wrong kind of women. None of their children amounted to as much as they did.

"Mother always held up to her boys the possibility of becoming President some day if they kept good habits", Col. Foster continued.

Although neither fate nor ambition happened to lead her boys in the direction of the Presidency, it did lead them along paths of honor and distinction in other fields. All six boys became merchants—with unusual records. Although they were exposed to the risks of mercantile life for many years, not one of them failed to pay one hundred cents on the dollar, Col. Foster stated.

So this mother of six sons, and this father also—who deserved the credit of picking out the mother of his boys—allowed their sons to leave the farm at 14 or thereabouts. At least they had reached the age when they might have been of some real assistance on the farm, near Newburgh on the Hudson, Orange County, N. Y., when they were allowed to start out in life.

David N. Foster began his career at the age of 14 as a bundle boy in New York City. In those days he recalled there was not a retail delivery wagon in New York. All deliveries were made on the backs of bundle boys. David was employed in the dry goods store of W. E. Lawrence, one of the old mer-

Colonel D. N. Foster at the age of 21 years. The photo was taken when he was home on furlough, recovering from a wound received at the Battle of Fredericksburg. Because of his wounded foot, he is standing on one leg holding on the chair for support.

chants of the city. Even at this time the firm did a large business.

This energetic bundle boy started to work at 7 o'clock in the morning and worked till 9 at night. In those days the stores in New York kept open until 11 o'clock on Saturday night.

"That is how I got my gait", Mr. Foster stated. "Mother told me that I would please my employer by hurrying as fast as I could when I set out on a delivery."

The gait had stayed with him at 89.

There was little of New York above Twenty-Third Street in 1856 when he started his career. The street-cars — horse-cars, of course — did run up Thirty-Second Street, but that was considered the outskirts of town. The salary for this job of bundle boy was $2.75 a week.

At 18, having saved some money out of his small salary, he went into business with his older brother, Scott Foster. The two brothers had a small retail dry goods business on Bleecker Street, between Commerce and LeRoy streets. They made a little money the first year. Their store had one clerk and two proprietors. Finally David decided to get a little education. His had been only the little red school house brand and not much of that. So he sold his interest in 1860 and entered the Montgomery Academy in Orange County to continue his education. This was about the beginning of the war.

"I remember the day my father came home from Newburgh and brought the news that Fort Sumter had been fired upon and that the President had called for 75,000 volunteers. I had been selected to make an address to my fellow students at the flag-raising on the following day. My first thought was that I would hold up to them the country's need for men. My next thought was that I couldn't do that without enlisting myself."

The result was that he was in the position of most heroes— he was literally forced into the role. His address consisted of a farewell to the students. That same afternoon he left by boat from Newburgh for New York to join the New York Ninth Militia. He was the first volunteer from Orange County. In a few days the regiment was off for Washington. The morning after they arrived, the regiment passed in review through the White House grounds, where they were reviewed by President Lincoln and General Winfield Scott who was still in command of the United States Army. The two stood on a horseblock as the reviewers stand, he recalled. And it was a bit crowded for the portly general and the tall thin President.

David Foster entered the Army as a private. We know him as Colonel. So there had to be quite a story right there. Until the Battle of Fredericksburg he served as a private and a non-com. In this battle on December 13, 1862, he was severely wounded in his right foot. He was taken to Washington City to the Government Hospital and the next morning five surgeons entered into an argument as to whether the foot should be amputated or not. Four held that he would die if the member was not taken off. The fifth said he might die even if it was. At this point the patient asked them to continue their conference elsewhere since they didn't give him a chance in the world.

So the young lieutenant—he had just been promoted—was left mercifully in the charge of the surgeon who did not want to see this young man lose his foot. And, of course, he got perfectly well and lived happily ever after.

"Have you been in the habit of drinking whiskey?", he was asked.

At the negative reply the surgeon said emphatically, "Then I'll be damned if your foot shall come off."

He recalled seeing Lincoln for the first time at a great meeting at Cooper Institute in New York City in February, 1860. At this time Lincoln made his greatest speech, he believed. At any rate, he was able to clinch his hold at the Chicago convention.

"If I ever believed in a special providence, it was on that occasion." Colonel Foster stated.

"New York and the East were all for Seward. And they were indignant at the choice of the convention. For Seward was the idol of the country."

He saw Lincoln next when, as president-elect, he was on his way to Washington for his first inauguration. He had taken a roundabout way because it was reported the Rebels were planning to wreck the presidential train. He saw Lincoln later when he visited the Army of the Potomac.

Colonel Foster confessed at this point that he had always had the scribbling itch. So in 1873, he went to Grand Rapids, Mich., and established the "Saturday Evening Post," a literary and news paper. At this time the now famous publication of that name was little known. At 32 he started this journalistic venture. The paper was destined to become the organ of the woman's suffrage movement in Michigan. The suffrage question was voted upon in Michigan in 1874.

The paper was a great success from the start. It attained quite a wide circulation. The editor had been converted to the cause of woman's suffrage under Henry Ward Beecher. He came to know well the great women leaders of the movement: Susan B. Anthony, Elizabeth Cady Stanton, Julia Ward Howe, Mary A. Livermore and Harriet Beecher Stowe.

"I value my association with those women more than anything in my lifetime", he said feelingly. "And the greatest of them all was Miss Anthony. Some day America ought to build a monument to her that will reach the skies.

"The prejudice against these women was so severe that they could not even come into the state of Michigan. Finally Miss Anthony was allowed to come, although there was no money to help her in her campaign. She hired her own hall and guaranteed her own expenses which she made by taking up a collection. She put more ginger into the campaign in 30 days than the rest of us had in months. She had the fervor of the evangelist in a good cause. And she paid her own way successfully. She knew her power and had no fear."

The Foster brothers by this time had dry goods stores in Evansville, Terre Haute, Fort Wayne and Grand Rapids, and two stores in New York City. They had found that they could make money best in the west. The Fort Wayne Store had been established on Columbia Street in 1868 as the New York City Store. David was persuaded to come to Fort Wayne and take charge of the store when his brother John's health failed.

Fort Wayne had a population of 14,000 at this time. On one side of a five-foot alley between Calhoun and Clinton Streets, on the south side of Columbia, was the New York Store, later Root and Company, and on the other side Foster brothers had their rival store. Both concerns made money rapidly in the prosperous new community.

"The ceilings were so low that you could almost touch them with your hands. And the landlords on Columbia Street never did anything but advance the rent everytime the lease expired. Fort Wayne was a one-street town. When these two stores left the street, they killed it for retail business", Col. Foster stated.

Then came the fight between Calhoun and Clinton streets as to which should be the business street of the city. The choice was to depend upon which was selected for a bridge over the St. Mary's River. The bridge was finally located on Clinton Street, but not before Foster brothers had made their choice of a business location—and the wrong choice as it turned out. They gambled on Clinton Street and it turned out Calhoun was the principal business street.

Even today, Colonel Foster pointed out, the Pennsylvania depot is more on Clinton than Calhoun. Even the officials of the railroad jumped the wrong way in their choice of a location. The direction a new town will take is often a gamble. There are several monuments of folly right in Fort Wayne proving how easy it is for even a shrewd man to guess wrong. The stock market is marked with just such follies.

Stores in those days would open at 6:30 o'clock to accommodate the line of farmers who had driven in with their grain by daylight to do their trading. They would buy a whole bolt of satinette, for instance, and mother would make up trousers and coats for all the children. The family would look like a young orphanage in uniform.

The most prominent pioneer merchants were Root and Company, Foster, and DeWald.

Throughout his life Colonel Foster was active in service to the community. He and Mrs. Foster were instrumental in putting through the legislature a bill in 1884 which provided for the first public library. As a result of this law the Fort Wayne Public Library was secured. The law empowered the school trustees to make a levy for the building and sustaining of public libraries. Practically all of the libraries of the state are a result of that act.

Colonel Foster commanded the Grand Army of the Republic

of the Department of Indiana in 1885 and was the senior past department commender for a great many years. He believed, however, that his service on the Park board from 1905 on, was of the greatest value to the community of any of his activities.

"I am in the harness at 89, and by the grace of God and Mayor Hosey I hope to die there", he said with real fervor.

If not, he would learn to play golf at 90. He had to do something to keep active. In fact, a few years before he had tried out against an experienced player and put the ball in the hole at a distance of 20 feet. Whereupon he was presented with a trophy—an empty coffee cup from which the grounds had just been drained.

He organized the company that laid out Lakeside, the first residential suburb. The low piece of land in the fork of the two rivers had lain there unimproved for over 100 years since the white man first came here. A group of men was called together by Col. Foster in the Pixley-Long block for a purpose that was not divulged until they arrived. As a result, the $250,000 capital was all subscribed before the meeting was over. The sum of $75,000 was paid for the 160 acres, and the first improved addition to the city was laid out.

Although there were two saloon keepers among the original stockholders, the important provision was made that there were to be no saloons in this district. This provision had been adhered to in all subsequent residence sections when we discussed the matter. It was the idea of Colonel Foster and others that saloons should be kept in the center of the city where they could be regulated, and not permitted in the rear of groceries where children were sent on errands.

On the first day of the sale of Lakeside lots, $182,000 worth of property was purchased. Little Lakeside was in a sense the pioneer grandmother of all the beautiful later residence additions. It is also one of the living monuments to Colonel Foster whose civic service was recognized during his lifetime by a handsome memorial statue in Swinney Park.

Of the many misplaced statues in Fort Wayne parks, it would seem that Colonel Foster's instead of General Lawton's would have been placed more suitably in the little Lakeside park area.

IX.
Country Girl Comes to the City

When Miss Isabelle Houghton, girl graduate of Defiance, Ohio, in 1881, travelled from the Wabash station down our best business street — Calhoun — it was paved with lumpy cedar blocks, lined on the east side by a low huddle of one-story buildings, with here and there on the west side a more pretentious two-story structure between vacant lots.

Eighty years ago Fort Wayne was still a small town, but the little country girls who came here were dismayed at their first sight of the city.

One took the street-car upon arriving — a one-horse, one-man car — with straw on the floor as a substitute for heat. And one passed 65 saloons between the Wabash station and the Court House. In fact, most of Calhoun Street was no place for a lady. For even the ladies who had to walk on the worn-out brick sidewalk on Calhoun Street took their courage in one hand and their long skirts in the other, and scooted to the best of their ability. It required the utmost care on the part of a lady pedestrian to keep from turning her ankle or breaking her neck.

Detzer's Drug Store, the second door north from Baker Street on Calhoun, was like a respectable oasis in a shabby desert. Calhoun Street, with its cedar blocks, was the only paved street in town. Clinton Street was a sea of mud. The postoffice was a one-story brick building on Court Street, which served as a dwelling as well.

As Mrs. Sam R. Taylor later, first curator of the Allen County-Fort Wayne Historical Museum, Miss Houghton was to know our city very well in the course of time.

In fact, it was after the story of Fort Wayne, the Indian village (Kikiyungi), the trading-post, the growing village, town and city had been preserved in both written and concrete form, in pictures, and relics — and up to the time this story was written, January 4, 1930 — all marked, labelled and arranged by the hand of Mrs. Taylor, that we discussed this fifty-year span of her busy career.

"The first water works system of Fort Wayne had just been put in operation in November, 1881. The first telephone system had been tried out unsuccessfully. The first electric arc lights had just been demonstrated satisfactorily by the Jenney Light Company," Mrs. Taylor recalled.

It was at this time that Judge Robert S. Taylor, brother of Sam R. Taylor, and father of Frank Taylor, geologist, was rising to national prominence. He had been appointed to a place on the Mississippi River Commission, the purpose of which was to control flood problems. He held this place for a third of a century. He also demonstrated his ability as a lawyer by defending successfully the Jenney patents; and was later retained by the government to defend the suit brought by Alexander Graham Bell for infringement on telephone patents in which he was also successful.

"The click of the first typewriter was not heard in the city until the summer of 1882," Mrs. Taylor recalled. "The Aveline Hotel, at the corner where the Tri-State Building stands now, was the only four-story building. The most pretentious retail business structure was the New York Store, now Rurode's. The Court House, built in 1861, was the only public building, with the exception of the school buildings, including the Jefferson, Clay, and High Schools.

"The finest theater the city afforded was the old skating rink, then called the Academy of Music, which stood on the site of the Standard Building on East Berry Street. There were many churches, but the only buildings with any architectural pretensions were the Methodist and Concordia Colleges. The corner stone of Library Hall, now the Central Catholic High School, had been laid the July preceding, but the old Masonic Temple was yet a dream.

"The great shops of the Pennsylvania Railroad regulated the clocks of a thousand employes. The Bass and Kerr Murray foundries, the Packard organ factory and the Centlivre brewery were the large industries of 1881. The Electric works was not built yet nor the Bowser plant or the Western Gas Company.

"The horse-cars had been in service about ten years at that

time. They were about twice as large as the station buses and were lighted by a single oil lamp which had to penetrate the small red eye of glass in the front end. Two springless seats extended down the sides. And the horses wore a doleful-toned bell to announce the approach of the car.

"If the stranger at the gates of the city hesitated to ride down town thus, he had the alternative of a worn-out brick sidewalk or of jolting in the bus over the decaying remains of a defunct Nicholson pavement," Mrs. Taylor said.

The car line had been extended as far as Fairfield Avenue to accommodate stockholders living in that exclusive suburb where there were 13 homes set in lovely natural grounds. Far beyond the border of the residence district were the organ factory and several smaller cottages. Some modest houses lay in the tract south of Creighton Avenue and east of Fairfield where the populous south side now lies.

The southeastern portion of the city was not opened to building until five years later when the part nearest the foundries and railroads was built up in spots. Hamilton's field on the edge of this section accommodated circuses until ten years later. The "West End" ended at the line of the old college campus and the fair grounds which is now Swinney Park. There was no Nebraska. Spy Run was inaccessible; Bloomingdale not much settled and Lakeside was undisturbed farmland.

Mrs. Taylor was identified with most of the pioneering ventures in which women had participated up to the 1930's. Her connection with the history of Fort Wayne as curator of the Allen County-Fort Wayne Historical Museum gave her an unusual opportunity to know about the city and county.

Fort Wayne has grown and there is a reason. In the first place, she points out the importance of its location. It is situated at a strategic point on the chief traffic route of the Northwest territory which was used by the Indians before local history begins. The past 50 years had witnessed the most tremendous development of transportation methods and equipment. The railroad brought shops. Other industries sprang into existence on account of the shipping facilities. Shops and industries brought men and families. The increase in population demanded greater food and fabric supplies. Commerce and housing accommodations were compelled to expand. And every form of expansion had taken place.

"In 1881 the east yards were creating a utilitarian suburb in the railroad district, necessary but most unlovely, and now taking its feet out of the mire, washing itself free from grime and becoming a locality of homes. The electric plant built on Broadway in 1882 demanded a home building movement in that quarter.

"The opening of the Bowser works for the manufacture of oil pumps in 1885 drew a part of the swelling population toward the southeast quarter, where farms were platted and streets opened. Between these two quarters, the land south of Creighton Avenue was suddenly needed for expansion of the great residential section of the city, and the plats were opened and swiftly bought up and built up following 1889. Swiftest of all the city expansions was the Lakeside suburb which was platted and sold in 1889, becoming a village almost overnight."

Other events which mark the progress of Fort Wayne, the rapidly growing city, were the coming of the electric street car lines from 1892 to 1894, the founding of the Wayne Knitting Mills in 1891, the opening of Robison Park by the Electric Railroad in 1806 and the Rolling Mills in 1902.

And that brought us up to the rapid real estate expansion of the 30 years of the 20th century, which was common knowledge. Natural gas had given great impetus to industries for the 15 years it was available.

It is the record of our earlier history that Mrs. Taylor deserved especial credit for preserving in the historical museum. There was scarcely a query about Fort Wayne after the coming of the first French explorers in the late seventeenth century that she cannot answer or locate information about. This local history in the concrete was being preserved in the museum. The Indian modes of living, the household equipment of the pioneers, customs, dresses, samples of the home arts such as quilting, carding, spinning, weaving are all preserved.

Customs, modes of living, civilization itself have changed, but as long as the Historical Museum remains, there is a tangible record of all that we have ever been beyond the time of which we have written records.

Baby bonnets, christening robes, bridal finery, calico and merino house dresses worn by pioneer mothers, and bearing the fine stitches put in by their busy fingers are mute evidence of their industry. The memory of dramatic incidents of our history — trying days in the Old Fort, Indians on the warpath, the French and British occupation — is preserved by the great iron key to the fort, the stone tomahawks, and arrowheads of the Indian, the French sabot, and metal weapons of British make.

Every item is meaningful; the least gadget has its place. It tells us how our forbears sanded their ink, kept their matches dry, lighted their fires and carded their wool, for their sturdy homespun garments.

On the walls are the oil portraits which were a veritable epidemic following the arrival of some eastern portrait painter to the new community. The slender, well-bred faces, the grave eyes, the blue-veined hands and simple finery are pictured in faithful colors.

"They were not just the rabble who settled in the fork of the rivers, but highly civilized and intelligent people, many of them of Revolutionary stock," Mrs. Taylor reminded me.

Of course, all the pioneering did not take place in the past centuries. The pioneer we have with us always. For pioneering is a habit of living with some people. The trail blazers are always ahead of the crowd. They walk before us, even today, leading the way.

The little Christmas seal that has become a symbol of health and hope in all parts of the world, had its local beginning in 1908. That year, Mrs. Taylor, assisted by Mrs. W. E. Davis and Miss Margaret Smith, conducted the first Red Cross Christmas Seal sale before the idea was taken over by the Anti-Tuberculosis League. The work was entirely volunteer work and the sale netted about $250,000. The idea was sponsored by the Woman's Club League.

The same year, the campaign for children's playgrounds was started by the civic committee of the Woman's Club League of which Mrs. Taylor was the chairman. The Better Yards movement which has attained such a great development today, had its humble origin in 1903 in the first distribution of seeds to school children under the direction of the Club League, with which Mrs. Taylor was identified as chairman at the time. Other pioneer movements sponsored by her were the public playgrounds and the high school cafeteria, both of which required publicity and the overcoming of opposition. Both movements were successful.

In the move to have women on the school board, Mrs. Taylor's presentation of the matter to the public and the city council, was endorsed by the Women's League as its expression of the case.

The history of Allen County's participation in World War I, the chapters on Allen County in Bert Griswold's Pictorial History of Fort Wayne were the work of Mrs. Taylor. The records of more than 4,000 soldiers of Allen County for the Council of Defense, used later in the Gold Star Book took her eleven months to prepare. The book on war work for the Fort Wayne Chapter of the American Red Cross was also her work.

The dramatic story of Angeline Chapoton, ancestress of Fort Wayne's first pioneer family, was told by her in the pageant presented by the Fort Wayne Historical Society on April 22, 1929. After 1923, Mrs. Taylor was in charge of all Allen County relics housed in the Court House until 1926 when they were removed to their permanent place in the old Swinney Homestead as the Allen County-Fort Wayne Historical Museum.

In this original collection, no matter how great it may grow, is the nucleus of a rich historic record that must continue intact and supply our descendants with all they may ever know about us and our pioneer culture. It is all the more needed for the reason that the belts of wampum on which our Indian predecessors on this spot recorded their history were destroyed by the white men in their first battle at this place.

X.

Great Days — the Sixties!

1

Although Mrs. Paul E. Wolf could not remember coming
from New York City where she was born, to Fort Wayne when
she was one year old, she had been told that they came by rail
from New York to Buffalo, by packet to Toledo, and on the
canal to Fort Wayne. It had all happened eighty years ago
when I talked with her in January, 1930.

Her grandfather had come from Germany in 1846 when
the trip in a sailing vessel took seventy days. Among the families when she came here with her parents were the Thiemes
and the Spiegels. Fort Wayne even then was a very promising
community, where thrifty and enterprising young people often
stopped for good on their way westward.

Julius Knothe, Mrs. Wolf's father, had a sawmill when the
only way the logs could be brought to him was on the canal.
When they came in 1850, they lived in Dr. Schmitz' house on
Calhoun Street near Wayne. Later they bought a lot on Jefferson Street, two blocks east of Calhoun, for $300. John N.
Miller, pioneer furniture dealer, lived across the street. The
Meyer family lived in the same block. Among the romances
of the time — or should we say three? — were the marriages
of the three Meyer girls to the three Berghoff boys who had
just come from Dortmund, Germany. Those were great days
— especially the sixties! Daniel Nestel, the father of Eliza
and Charlie Nestel — known throughout the world as the
midgets "Commodore Foote" and "Fairie Queen" — built next
door to them. The Tresselts built next door to the Nestel's.

Mrs. Wolf's father worked for Benjamin Tower, contractor.
When money was scarce, he would be paid with a due-bill instead of cash. The due-bill, moreover would have to be ex-
changed for whatever he could get at the store. One day he
came home with an armful of milk crocks — all he could get
with his due-bill — much to his wife's disgust.

"But we had a good time and it didn't cost so much," Mrs.
Wolf recalled.

They used to go to Colerick's Hall on Columbia Street to see the magic-lantern show, the forerunner of the movies. Then the circus used to come to town once a year and that was a great occasion.

As she talked she could see the wood back of Lewis Street where friends of the Knothe's lived; and far to the south was William's Grove. When she was five years old, little Miss Knothe attended a log parochial school on Barr Street. "I remember when there was a field at Harmar and Maumee Avenue and one day I climbed the fence and lost my scissors there."

The Concordia College students made a walk of two planks from the college grounds through the fields to Harmar Street. She recalled the custom of taking students into the homes for Sunday dinner. Every family had their "student," as they called him, at one time or another. This provided a home atmosphere for the boy away from home. The family would even take care of the student's laundry and keep his clothes mended.

The "student" in the Knothe family was Martin Luecke, for many years president of Concordia. Many romances resulted from the custom. For the daughter of the family in many instances, would set her cap for the student, who, it might be added, proved a willing victim.

Among the notable older Concordia faculty men who were friends of the Knothe's were Professor Martin Schick, and Dr. W. G. Sihler, for many years the pastor of St. Paul's Lutheran Church. Dr. Sihler had laid the foundation for the entire Lutheran Synod, Mrs. Wolf said. He had been a nobleman in the old country, and had changed his name from Alexander, the pagan and militaristic name, to William when he went into the ministry.

And the ague! That was a bitter memory. Quinine by the gross was administered. The victim shook one day with chills, and burned the next with fever.

At one time Knothe and Griebel had a furniture store on the alley back of the present location of the Schlatter Hardware Company. The building was a white frame. During an epidemic of cholera they had to turn their attention to making coffins. They also had the only hearse in town.

The plagues of that day were due to lack of sanitation, no

Above at left shows Paul E. Wolf at the age of 21, just before coming to this country from Dresden in 1871. Mrs. Wolf, as Miss Marie Knothe, in 1873, at right.

The first home of Mr. and Mrs. Wolf, on East Wayne Street, near Monroe, where they lived following their marriage in 1874, is shown in the photo above.

doubt. One year everyone was afraid to eat the peaches and cucumbers for fear of disease, and the entire crop had to be dumped into the river.

Among the early merchants were the Root Store, later Rurode's, which started on Columbia Street. DeWald's Retail Dry Goods Store stood where the wholesale house stood later at Columbia and Calhoun. The Wolf upholstering business was established in 1873 on Calhoun Street where the Colonial

Theater stood later, near the corner of Washington and Calhoun. Later the store was removed to Clinton Street in the Miner Block, which Mr. Wolf purchased of the Ewing estate some years later. The town had a population of 16,000 when he started his business.

There were no clerks in this store as in most of the early places of business. It was assumed that everyone was perfectly honest and they waited on themselves. It was the beginning of the cash-and-carry plan before the elaborate telephone, charge-account commercial era.

Mrs. Wolf remembered Ewing's Grove where Ewing Street is now, and Taylor's apple orchard across from Concordia. There were cornfields near Calhoun Street no farther away than Harrison. The Bonds lived far out on Fairfield, with fields between their home and the city, where Beechwood Circle is now.

New York seemed far away. But uncles in New York used to send books to the Knothe home — the like of which could not be bought in Fort Wayne. When Mrs. Wolf was 18 she went to New York on a visit lasting five months. It was a marvelous experience for that time.

Mr. and Mrs. Wolf were married by Rev. Sihler in 1874. They have had sixteen children, thirteen of whom lived to manhood and womanhood. Theirs was a real pioneer family. They started life together in a little one-story frame house at 180 East Wayne Street in what is now the 500 block.

In building the family home on Canal Street, they used joists of solid hand-hewn oak from the old St. Paul's school building, which are the despair of electricians and all other workmen to this day. A library table of generous dimensions in their home was made of an oaken log that had lain in the Feeder Canal, and had belonged to R. C. Bell. A great walnut bookcase had once belonged to Judge Coombs.

A miniature chest was made by Mr. Wolf's father as an engagement present to his mother in Germany. It was necessary for a young man in Germany at that time to demonstrate his skill as a craftsman before he could be considered fully educated. It was also well to prove to the young lady of his choice that he had this skill.

One thing is certain — the thrifty Germans who came to this

country in the middle of the last century could never foresee in their wildest dreams the day a man had to become a criminal to get a drink!

A directory of 1875-76 told in 300 pages all there was to know about the population and industries of Fort Wayne in 1875. Mr. Wolf was fond of turning the pages that told him a story of progress, and recorded Fort Wayne's growth and achievements. It also gave clues to the business customs of that day.

Paul Wolf's ad showed a cut of the haircloth sofa and high-backed chair so fashionable then. He dealt in "fine uphol-stered furniture, lounges, sofas, tete-a-tetes," et cetera. Particu-lar attention was given to the repair of church cushions, which, it seemed, were used frequently enough to wear out at that time.

Full-page ads were devoted to bottled beer, ale and porter, "expressly for family use." The Washington Street Brewery at the corner of Washington and Wabash Avenue, was pic-tured with a wooden rail fence and pleasant shade trees in the yard.

L. Fortriede was a dealer in boots and shoes at 32 West Main Street. George Biemer was a manufacturer of all kinds of wagons and open buggies. F. Foellinger was proprietor of the "Pioneer Boot and Shoe Store." Men at that time wore boots that pulled on.

S. A. Aurentz had a grocery at 137 Broadway. I. Knapp and Son were dentists on the southwest corner of Berry and Clinton Streets. L. O. Hull, painter, was in business at 75 Calhoun Street. F. P. Randall was attorney, land and insur-ance agent with a capital of $17,000,000. Fred J. Hayden was a real estate and insurance broker with an office with Samuel T. Hanna next door to the postoffice.

A handsome cabinet organ was pictured in the ad of the Fort Wayne Organ Company, manufacturers of the Packard orches-tra organ, with S. B. Bond as president, J. D. Bond, treasurer and G. W. Bursley, secretary and manager.

Seven Colericks — David H., Edward F., Henry, Thomas, Philemon B., and Walpole, attorneys, and John A. Colerick — were listed.

The name Hamilton occurred twenty-two times and Hanna eleven times.

The Hedekin House offered accommodations at $1.50 a day. Commodious stabling for horses was also offered.

Alfred Hattersley was a plumber and gas fitter at 48 East Main Street. Hoffman Brothers were manufacturing articles of black walnut lumber in the sawmill at 300 West Main Street. Hiram C. Moderwell and George S. Fowler were shirtmakers at the corner of Calhoun and Berry.

There were three florists, four flour mills, eight furniture manufacturers and dealers, one gold and silver plater, two pages of insurance agents, two laundries, four music teachers, ten newspapers, daily and weekly, one bus line, two paperhangers, one pawn broker, one portrait painter — Joseph Dille — one produce dealer, and 85 saloons. Yes, I counted them!

The newspapers, lest you may doubt my word as I doubted my own eyes, were the Daily News, Fort Wayne Gazette, and Fort Wayne Sentinel, daily; Indiana Staats-Zeitung, tri-weekly; Fort Wayne Courier, Fort Wayne Gazette, Fort Wayne Journal, and Fort Wayne Sentinel, weeklies; Indiana Staats-Zeitung and Indiana Volksfreund, weekly.

An analysis by experts, showing Fort Wayne's early tendencies and its line of development at the three-quarters of a century mark, would be interesting. But that would be another story.

2

"See that black hill over yonder! That is the way America will look when you get there. A wilderness!"

With the accumulated wisdom of her years, Grandmother Kraft was trying to make her eager young people realize the disadvantages of life in the new world. They were more than comfortable in their neat home in a little village in Hanover, Germany. They had pride in their province, too. Years later they pointed out that Hanover had been the native province of Prince Albert, who became the consort of Queen Victoria. They were even proud of him.

Grandmother Kraft's warnings were not heeded. The little family which consisted of William Schrader, his wife, her parents and three brothers made the long trip to America. I got the story from a son, H. C. Schrader, now deceased, who was born on October 23, 1837, in Hardin County, Ohio, three years after his parents had made the trip.

The land they lived on in Germany had been under cultivation for centuries. There was no pioneering to be done there. Only the distant wooded hills were covered with dark forests. Grandmother was the only one who knew anything about life in a wilderness. She was not eager to risk its perils again..

The Napoleonic wars and their devastation were within the memory of the young people of 1830. Many a young man had gone forth never to return. Among these was the grandfather of Mr. Schrader. It was no wonder that the new world was a land of promise in those days.

There were high hopes in the hearts of the little band of German immigrants. The promised land offered all they wanted in this life, they thought. The trip from Bremen to Baltimore took six weeks. The newcomers went first to Wheeling, W. Virginia, and then pushed further into the wilderness of Ohio. For wilderness it truly was. Not a tree had been felled where they stopped.

"People today don't know what it was like to settle in a new country. For three years we lived on corn bread. We had nothing else. There were no plows. So we had to dig with a hoe after the trees were felled and the land cleared. Then we planted corn."

William Schrader had been a mechanic — a wagon maker in Germany. So he pursued his trade in the new country where there was great need for wagons. He made covered wagons, the kind that went across the overland trails and carried the prospectors to California in '49. He was all set to make the trip with his family when something occurred to prevent it. Mr. Schrader, who was a boy of 12, can't quite remember what. Maybe it was a new baby.

There were six children in the family. They attended the county schools in Hardin County during those early days and sat on slab benches that were made with the bark left on the underside. There was no danger of snagging children's stockings in those days. Homespun clothes and wool socks could stand most any rough contact, even bark lined benches, without noticeable wear and tear.

They made their own candles, the tallow dips used for lights.

A mold held six candles. The tallow was poured into the mold and allowed to harden around the wick.

Travel in those days was by coach before the railroad was put through. In a few years after they settled in Hardin County, the town of Kenton was established and it was the terminus of the Mad River railroad. He remembered the first train to arrive in Kenton. His father took the children to see the great galloping engine. He was about ten years old at the time. This was a memorable occasion because they also heard the click of the telegraph then for the first time.

One of the pictures that has never faded from his memory is a stampede of cattle. A shipment of cattle was going through Kenton on foot when a storm came up. The cattle became frightened and started to run. He never forgot the sound of those terrified pounding hoofs which seemed to go on forever.

"Hardin County, hard work, that's what it meant," his mother used to say. Grandmother had been right about it. Although there was no time for vain regrets. All they could do was to pitch in and work to settle the new country. Gradually the memory of their native Hanover and Prince Albert faded into a dim tradition, to be perpetuated in the name of a frock coat which became the fad in the civilized parts of the new world.

"Calhoun Street was paved with planks from the railroad to Main Street, when I came here in 1866," Mr. Schrader recalled. "There was only one farm house south of the Wabash and Pennsylvania railroads. A fine modern cedar block pavement was put down in later years. The best building in town was the Keystone Block at the corner of Calhoun and Columbia Streets. The building is standing today (1930). It was occupied by the Nirdlinger Clothing Store, Meyer Brothers Drug Store, Keil Book Store, the Falk Clothing Store, Lamley and Rosenthal Cigar Store, MacDougal and Shoaff Carpet Store. The George DeWald Store stood on the location of the present DeWald Wholesale House.

"Columbia Street was the principal business street in those days, and there were flourishing business houses down to the canal, which ran parallel with the Nickel Plate tracks. Because they were unable to buy the land for the railroad right-of-way, the builders of the road stole a march on the canal owners.

They filled in the canal from Clinton to Calhoun Street on a Sunday and thus got possession of it."

Hamilton Hall stood where Rurode's stands today. Colerick's Hall on Columbia Street was the popular opera house.

Strange to say, Mr. Schrader did not feel that the old times were the best. Throughout his later years he had held out a goal for his span of life. That goal had kept him young and in touch with events. He wanted to live to see woman's suffrage accomplished. Then he hoped to see national prohibition put into effect. Both hopes were realized.

He cast his first vote for Lincoln in 1861 and his second vote for him in 1865. He remained a consistent Republican ever after in all presidential elections. He had cast his last vote for Hoover.

His chief enthusiasm was prohibition. Throughout his life he was associated with the prohibition party except in national elections. His temperance convictions went back to his early boyhood. He could not remember a time when he did not feel strongly on the subject.

"When I came to Fort Wayne there was a saloon in every square on Calhoun Street. You can't tell me that we aren't better off today than we were in the old saloon days.

"I have always believed with the late ex-President Taft who said that if we ever got light wines and beer, there would be a place to sell them. In that case the saloon would come back.

"I have one criticism to make of the temperance workers. When the Eighteenth amendment was passed, they seemed to rest from their labor and call it good. There was no longer any effort made to educate against liquor. More intelligent effort was made in the direction of education against the liquor traffic in the past than in any other phase of temperance work."

Among the early workers in the cause of temperance in this community were Judge Taylor and Judge Ninde. Meetings were held in the Princess Rink in the old days, he recalled.

"I have not a word of commendation for the liquor traffic," he said with some heat. "It is the meanest, dirtiest piece of business men ever indulged in. Europe would like to get rid of their liquor traffic. I have always had a high regard for the Ladies Home Journal because of the stand they took against liquor in an early day."

In spite of the discouraging look of the liquor situation of that time, Mr. Schrader did not believe in giving in an inch to the powers working against enforcement. He could see the argument advanced by some that sufficient time was not given to those who had all of their means tied up in the liquor business at the time the amendment was put into effect. Better results might have been obtained if more time had been given to dispose of their property and a better feeling might have been the result. He admitted the truth of the argument.

But the liquor traffic, per se, has always been a menace to any community or country. It always worked degradation on individuals and the community, he thought, and there never was anything that could be said for it. The wave of lawlessness that followed national prohibition only proved how fearful and desperate this force is when it is thwarted. He hoped to see the day when prohibition would be even more rigidly enforced.

However, it wasn't such a bad world, after all, Mr. Schrader believed. Nor did he think it was growing any worse. He was so interested to know what was coming next that he had no time to think about coming to the end of a long life. At ninety-three one has lived a fairly long time. The changes that had come were so perfectly amazing that he could only guess at what was yet to come. He didn't want to miss any of it. It is that healthy curiosity that he believed was responsible more than anything else for his length of days.

XI.

Good Cheer Came Cheap

1

Hospitality and good cheer did not come so high in the days when whiskey was 25 cents a gallon and room and board in Fort Wayne's best hostelry — the Hedekin House — could be had for $4 a week.

Ely G. Anderson, Civil War veteran and merchant, came to Fort Wayne from Ohio in 1846 at the age of seven. His father, Calvin Anderson, had been keeper of the famous Red Brick Tavern between Columbus and Springfield, Ohio. As manager of the flourishing Hedekin House on Barr Street, Ely had watched Fort Wayne grow from a mere village of 1500 for quite a number of years.

Among the taverns when he came was Washington Hall on the southeast corner of Barr and Columbia Streets, convenient for passengers arriving on the canal boats. The building was built by the Ewings, and Peter Timmons was an early landlord. The Spencer House stood across from the Court House on Calhoun Street. The Post Tavern was located on Columbia between Clinton and Calhoun.

The bar was at this time an essential in every first-class hotel. Men traveled long distances on horseback and would come into the warmth of a tavern and demand something to cheer and stimulate them. But Mr. Anderson did not hold with this idea even in the early days.

"If I can't run a hotel without a bar, I won't run it at all," he said.

However, when a man came to him after a long drive and asked for "something to warm a fellow up," he was the generous host. He kept a supply of whiskey in his bedroom, and would invite his guests in and GIVE them the liquor. In those days it cost 25 cents a gallon and a man could afford to be generous.

Lewis Street was the city line on the south at that time. Most of the business firms were situated within a few blocks on

Columbia Street. The packets landed at the foot of Barr Street and the principal business street naturally ran parallel with the canal. The Nickel Plate Railroad follows the road-bed of the canal. Ely Anderson used to put up groceries for the packet when he was a young man.

If he had the artist's gift he would have been able to sketch from memory every foot of the way in downtown Fort Wayne. The Pennsylvania Railroad laid its tracks down Lafayette

The picture above shows narthwest corner of Calhoun and Main Streets in the sixties when the building where the Citizens Trust Company stands now was occupied by Anderson and Ely, grovers, and the Merchants National Bank. The photograph is the property of E. G. Anderson, 2409 Calhoun Street, pioneer merchant and Civil War veteran. He was engaged in the grocery business with his father, Calvin Anderson, when the Civil War was declared.

Street when it came in 1854, and the depot stood where Weil Brothers stood for many years. The packet landing was near the Comparet Warehouse at Columbia and Barr Streets. The Hedekin House stood just where it stands today on Barr, near Columbia.

Nearby were Michael Hedekin's Grocery and 10 shanties for the Irish who were employed in digging the canal. Nearby was the candy store mentioned by several old-timers where they watched the owner pull his candy and spit on his hands to give vim and vigor to his task.

The places of business on Columbia Street that he remembered, said Mr. Anderson were Simonton's Bakery near Clinton, John Moore's Shoe Store, a grocery kept by Monjean, a Frenchman; D. W. Burroughs' Bookstore, the Misses Wells' Millinery Shop, Charlie Hardeman's Barber Shop, Probasco Tailor Shop, Coombs' Bakery and dwelling, A. L. Johns' Saddlery, kept by the father of A. L. Johns and Miss Mallie Johns, at the corner of Calhoun and Columbia.

On the north side of Columbia Street was the store of Samuel Hanna at Barr and Columbia, James Walker's Drug Store and Cottrell's Restaurant and Saloon, D. W. Bowen's Saddlery Shop, Morris Cody's Grocery and L. P. Stapleford's auction room. A French family by the name of Vallecat lived in a frame dwelling in this block next to C. M. Wells' feed barn where the hay and oats were sold to feed the canal horses. Next was Beecher's Drug Store, then Schwieter's Bakery. Where the Clark Fruit Company formerly stood, Peter P. Bailey had a hardware store. He was one of the founders of the Episcopal Church. The second floor was occupied by the G. W. Woods' Printing office, and the first telegraph office in town.

G. W. Wood was the town's first mayor, whose residence is still standing on the corner of Superior and Wells Streets. It must be remembered that Superior Street was Water Street at that time and had many fine residences, of which the home of Hugh McCulloch, now the Turnverein club house, is standing today.

"The only mean trick I ever played on anyone was to leave my father when the war started. I had just gone into the grocery business with him," Mr. Anderson admits with some regret. But the call to arms had to come first with every loyal young patriot.

The firm of Anderson and Ely, Grocers, stood at the corner of Calhoun and Main Streets where the Citizens Trust Company located later. The Court House Square, he points out, was the location that was admirably selected and has remained just where it is today. On one corner there was a log jail. The little frame Court House was not large enough for all the county offices even at that time. So Alex Wiley, the treasurer, built a two-story office building for John Conger, the clerk.

In the early days before the Civil War, Mr. Anderson recalled only two houses on Wayne Street. They were the residences of Louis Woelke on Wayne and Calhoun, and Dr. C. S. Schmitz, the father of Mrs. Douglass, deceased. Dr. Schmitz was a well-known figure and drove a white horse and phaeton. A frame church stood where the Cathedral of the Immaculate Conception stands today, when Father Julian Benoit was the priest.

Ely Anderson attended a private school where the City Light office stands now on East Berry Street. It was taught by Mrs. Rowan, the mother of Mrs. J. B. Harper, deceased. He also attended Alexander McJunkin's School in a little frame building that stood on Lafayette Street between Berry and Wayne. His education was finished in the East End School or old Clay School.

Among his relics are several copper pennies that were struck off for advertising purposes by local business houses. One is for the Twelve Mile House of which George Metzger was the proprietor. Another was for C. Anderson, dealer in groceries and provisions, dated 1864. A page is devoted to shinplasters, worth about $2, in his scrap-book of Civil War mementoes.

"People today don't realize what it meant to be a soldier. And especially what it meant to us in the Civil War to have to fight hand to hand with young Americans. It was awful, of course. Nobody wants war less than a soldier. But I believe in preparedness. Not being prepared only makes it worse."

While playing the old reed organ as substitute organist in a church in Nashville after the war, Mr. Anderson met Miss Sarah Jane Wilson who sang in the choir. It was in this way the romance started in 1865. With his southern bride he remained in Nashville as a street car conductor.

His scrap-book, however, provides a record of the social customs in early Fort Wayne. New Year's was observed in a hospitable, yet stately manner in the homes. More formal affairs were held in the hotels. A "New Year's Soiree" in the old Rockhill House in 1858 was given with the compliments of the managers, and all the lively young men in town whose names were on the invitations as the hosts. Among them were John H. Bass, Charles McCulloch, Fred J. Hayden, among others. As "Rockhill's Folly," the building which became a part of St. Joseph's Hospital, was known because of its unfortunate location. Michael Hedekin had guessed right when he built in the center of the thriving part of the community, near to the canal landing.

A copy of the Fort Wayne Morning Gazette for April 15, 1878, gives a detailed account of Mr. and Mrs. Calvin Anderson's golden wedding. At this time fashionable bonnets could be purchased for $1.50. Short walking dresses were rapidly becoming popular with the ladies — "and the gents" — the editor observed.

The scale of prices of that day included imported nuts at 15 cents a quart and oysters from 10 to 20 cents a can. Breakfast bacon was nine cents and pickled pork six cents a pound.

Coffee A and coffee C, sugar, granulated and powdered sugar were seven, eight, nine and ten cents a pound. Fine cut and plug tobacco, without which no grocery could do business, were 40 and 50 cents a pound.

The editorial cliches of the time included such items as these: Bayard Taylor was on the bounding billows on his way to Europe. Murat Halstead of the Cincinnati Commercial was on the briny deep also bound thitherward. Mrs. Van Cott was dead bent on preaching, and had declared that neither John Wesley nor St. Paul himself could stop her.

Good accommodations for man and beast were advertised at local taverns. Board and room could be had as low as $3.50 per week. "Hired girls" were being paid $1.50 per week.

The advertising columns contained many inches of ads for lawyers and railroads. Among the lawyers were the firms of Aldrich and Barrett, Jenison and Alden, and F. P. Randall. Two rival millinery firms engaged in villification of each other in paid ads. Paul Wolf and Company were engaged in the upholstery business at 51 East Main Street at that time.

The Louisiana State Lottery "incorporated by the Legislature of the State for Educational and Charitable purposes in 1868" offered a splendid "opportunity to win a fortune." The fifth grand distribution was held Tuesday, May 14, New Orleans, La.

Dress materials in cotton cost from twelve and a half cents, or a shilling, up to 20 cents. Eggs were eight cents a dozen, potatoes 25 cents a bushel and butter 20 cents per pound.

Needless to add, these were called the good old days!

2

The intersection of Calhoun and Berry Streets was so far out of the center of business a century ago that it was not considered proper for a lady to go there unaccompanied.

Even the site of the First National Bank was outside of the business district in 1854 when Captain William Kelsey, of 515 Lawton Place, came to Allen County at the age of 12. The business center was concentrated in a block or two along Columbia Street at that time.

"I remember going to the Townley store where the DeWald Company was located later, with my mother when we had just come here from Rush County. My mother asked to be directed to a good millinery store. Mr. Townley told her to go to Mrs. Sulley's little shop in a one-story building where the First National Bank now stands. But he said it was so far out of the business district that he would accompany her to be sure she arrived there safely."

The new community was beset with rough and picturesque characters, we are told. All of the earliest settlers had to be hardy adventurers and had to come either by horseback or by pirogue on the river. Sea captains, Indian traders, pioneer merchants and restless adventurers of every ilk made up the early population. The better element stayed and built up the town while the idle and useless moved on to greener pastures eventually.

Captain Kelsey's busy career has covered many dramatic periods in the history of Fort Wayne and Indiana. One of the interests of his later years was to trace his own family tree back to William Kelsey, the common ancestor of all the Kelseys, who came to this country and settled in New Towne, Mass., in 1633, just one year after its founding.

The founder of the American branch of the family was born in Sussex County, England, in about the year 1600. After stopping in New Towne near Boston, which is now Cambridge, he and his family became dissatisfied and moved on to Connecticut where they established another New Towne, near Hartford. The name of William Kelsey is engraved on a tall granite shaft as one of the founders of Hartford.

Successive generations moved into New Jersey. Then Thomas Kelsey, great-grandfather of Captain Kelsey, came westward to Mason County, Kentucky. His children came to Ohio in 1800 and their descendants are now scattered throughout this state and adjoining states. James Kelsey is the immediate ancestor of nearly all the Indiana members of the family.

Captain Kelsey was born in Rush County, Indiana, in 1842, and came to Aboite Township, Allen County, in 1854.

In the early days in Fort Wayne, Captain Kelsey attended the Methodist College where he was a classmate of General Henry W. Lawton. He recalled vividly the days of the canal. In fact, he was part owner and had charge of the last canal boat that came through the aqueduct. And, of course, he was a member of the Aqueduct Club, a democratic organization of men who were once just boys together, swimming in the old aqueduct — Fort Wayne's old swimming hole.

He recalled the days of the Spencer House, Fort Wayne's leading hostelry before the coming of the railroad. It stood opposite the Court House square. It preceded the Hedekin House, still standing on Barr Street, which became the important hotel after the coming of the railroad. The first engine that ever came into the city, he said, came knocked down and was put together in the Comparet warehouse and commission house which stood on Columbia and Barr Streets.

The four old families he recalled as the earliest to settle and become prominent were the Allen Hamilton family, the Edsall, the Hanna and the Comparet families.

Allen Hamilton, the great merchant of this section, was a great friend of Richardville, the Indian chieftian, so well-known to the early settlers. In fact, a man's success in those days depended largely upon his ability to understand and deal with the Indian who held the valuable land by right of occupation.

On one occasion, Allen Hamilton was riding a very fine spirited horse along Columbia Street, when he met Richardville. The story goes something like this::

"Ho, Mr. Hamilton!"

"Ho! Richardville!"

"I strike on that horse, Mr. Hamilton."

Mr. Hamilton at once alighted, and handed over his fine horse to its future owner, according to Indian custom.

Some time later, the Chief and Mr. Hamilton were riding together along the Wabash, where the Chief had several fine reservations of land.

"Chief, I strike on this section."

"Well," said the chief, "I make you a deed for it, but we'll not strike any more."

The most dramatic incident occurred when his regiment, the Forty-fourth Indiana, gathered on a fine fall day in 1861, while all the citizens thronged the streets of Fort Wayne to watch the pageant of officers and men in new uniforms. The regiment was composed of fresh-faced country lads, most of them in their teens. They were stalwart and strong, somewhat larger in stature than the native-born Hoosier. Many of them had come west with their parents in the general trek from Ohio, Pennsylvania, New York, and the eastern states. Such youths!

They formed a hollow square on the Court House square and were addressed by Mayor Franklin P. Randall. At the same time, a beautiful silk American flag, the gift of the citizens of Fort Wayne, was presented to the regiment. Concluding his address, Mayor Randall followed the words of the marriage ceremony and required the men to promise to love, honor, and obey the flag and to sustain and defend it even unto death. Answers were given in the affirmative to his questions and he concluded with these words:

"I then, in the presence and before these witnesses, solemnly join you to the American flag; and what we have now joined together let not Jeff Davis or his minions put asunder."

The regiment went to Indianapolis and on down to slave territory where they served in the Green River campaign, the siege of Fort Henry, the battle of Shiloh, and at Fort Donelson, until at last the flag was shot to pieces. But the tattered remnants were returned to the citizens of Fort Wayne as a pledge of faith and loyalty, stained with the blood of thirty-nine men who gave their lives to defend it.

Captain Kelsey was paralyzed in the legs early in the war. After a partial recovery he went back into the Army of the Shenandoah and served until the war was over.

He remembers distinctly when the free school became effective in Allen County. He attended the first free school in the county in Aboite Township in the winter of 1854 and 1855. There were fifty pupils enrolled in the school which was held in an old log dwelling.

Many were the arguments put up by the enemies of the system who pointed out the great injustice to the childless man who would be made to support his neighbors' "little brats." This, he said, was brotherly love in the fifties!

Indiana's reputation for schools was built largely on the tradition of Edward Eggleston's "Hoosier Schoolmaster," he believed. Before the free schools were established, only those children were educated whose parents could see the advantage of paying out money for something of uncertain value in a new world.

In summing up, Captain Kelsey pointed out that the early associations are the lasting ones. The old Aqueduct and Civil War memories are nearest to his heart. He held at one time or other all the offices in the Bass-Lawton Post. He served as junior vice department commander, and on the national council of administration, and department commander of Indiana in 1922 and 1923.

His most valued treasures are the records of the Allen County soldiers in the war of the Rebellion from 1861 to 1865. One page of the great book of personal records is filled with bona-fide Confederate money.

"If there was to be a fire I'd grab first for my pants and next for these books. I keep them at the foot of my bed always," Captain Kelsey said.

A soldier, a scholar and a gentleman was Captain Kelsey, with an attitude of genuine respect and reverence for God, country, flag and home that was unswerving. In fact the old-fashioned courtesy of the men of his generation would be hard to match in any era.

XII.
Fort Wayne's Greenwich Village

Fort Wayne has had its Greenwich Village. In the middle of the last century, not long after the Civil War, Fort Wayne had its artist colony. Perhaps it did not ramble through as many squares and alleys as New York's Greenwich Village; but it had many of the earmarks of a little Bohemia.

The George W. Wood house on the corner of Wells and Superior Streets was the home of a group of artists and writers. The Fort Wayne colony was privileged to live in the spacious home of George W. Wood, first mayor of Fort Wayne, after his death when his widow turned it into an exclusive family hotel.

"We were really members of the first official family," Mrs. Carrie M. Shoaff, who lived in the little colony for thirteen years, recalled with pride.

Mrs. Shoaff's special brand of art was a process of making pottery to resemble Limoges ware. Among the residents were playwrights, magazine writers, and portrait painters.

"The old house ran back to the St. Mary's River," Mrs. Shoaff recalled as she produced a faded picture of the place. "Here was my studio in the basement, a huge room originally intended as a dining-room. It had great wide window sills and a cheery fireplace. The pottery was down at the river's edge, right in view of the old aqueduct. The old Dutch potter would listen to our instructions with eyes as expressionless as blue marbles and then turn out perfect work. He knew how, all right, even if he didn't look it."

A group of Mrs. Shoaff's pottery bore witness to the transforming power of the potter's hand. Common river mud had been converted by the artist, even without a kiln or potter's wheel, by a process invented by Mrs. Shoaff. This process achieved a certain degree of fame in that early day and gained for its originator a place in a book called "Women of the Century,"by Frances Willard and Mary Livermore. A picture of the artist and a sketch of her work was included among the

Mrs. Carrie M. Shoaff, nee Gifford, Artist and Author

actresses, temperance workers, advocates of women's rights, writers and artists.

One other Fort Wayne woman to be honored in a similar way was Mrs. Caroline Woodward, a magazine writer and painter, also a member of the colony. Other distinguished names familiar to their generation were those of Ada Rehan, Fanny Davenport, Elizabeth Cady Stanton and May Wright Sewell. The book appeared in 1893 with 1400 sketches of distinguished women in every walk of life.

"I firmly believe that the book did more to help the cause of women than anything that was ever accomplished in my time," was the deep conviction of Mrs. Shoaff, a pioneer in many fields.

In the first place, soon after her marriage to U. S. Shoaff in

1869, she brought down on her head the wrath of the straight-laced members of the community by serving as a clerk in her husband's department store in Huntington. "A woman has no right to loaf in her husband's place of business," was the sentiment expressed by the men of the family.

She was the first woman reporter in Fort Wayne in the seventies. Her cards printed at that time identify her as "Correspondent, Fort Wayne Gazette." A letter written to her just after she arrived in New York to write special letters for the paper, has as its letterhead a graphic map of Fort Wayne, then a town of 40,000 inhabitants, the hub of the middlewest. The courteous letter was written by Rosser McClure, managing editor of the Gazette at that time.

"Many is the time I praised a bum railroad in those days to pay for the pass that was granted to the press," she commented. In those days the courtesy of the railroads and hotels was extended to members of the profession. From her headqquarters at the Sturtevant Hotel, at that time a family hotel, she conducted her business of meeting and interviewing prominent people. Among them was Mary Gay Humphreys, of Fort Wayne, a contributor to Harper's Bazaar and other periodicals.

A pottery class had been organized for Mrs. Shoaff in New York when fate took a hand, and illness delayed her realization of this plan.

Here to the Fort Wayne colony came Alice B. Torrance, a bride of 17, who accompanied her husband to South America when he was United States consul to Brazil. She wrote her account of the thrilling trip in rooms opening on a balcony on the second floor. A portrait of Mrs. Torrance in Spanish lace was painted by her brother, Ed Edmondson, another member of the group.

There was George MacManus of Howe, Indiana, "the Farmer Poet," popular lecturer, entertainer and friend of Bill Nye. Mrs. Isaac D'Isay, then Alida Morss, was also one of the group. Her claim to fame was as a contributor to the Mid-Continent Magazine, especially on an assignment to interview the late Bishop Quale. Her mother, Mrs. Susan Hill Morss, has been credited with being the first school-teacher in Fort Wayne, in a room where Bruder & Calhoun's Jewelry Store stood, and where Murphy's Store stands today.

"Mart Spencer was the owner of the Fort Wayne Gazette, and he was the one who got me to write chatty letters for the paper. I remember when he came back from the Civil War with his face all sawed up with bias cuts. He used to come over to the Wood House to see the bunch. In those days a Sunday article brought about $2.00."

Newspaper reporters in those days wore full beards, she recalled.

Into this colony came Joseph Arthur, actor, from New York, as a guest of the Wood House. After making his first appearance as the hind legs of an elephant in company with Henry S. Dixie as the front legs, he had gone on to better things. His current ambition was to put on plays in Fort Wayne, the first of which was to be "The Still Alarm," a dramatization of Ballantine's novel. Mrs. Shoaff was engaged to write the lines of the play.

"I mailed my first manuscript at the local postoffice with a sinking heart as it was to be criticized by the eminent critic, A. C. Wheeler, who wrote under the pen name of "Nim Crinkle." He was a cousin of Ella Wheeler Wilcox, and he used to say what a fool she was to write those red flannel poems of passion of hers," Mrs. Shoaff continued.

The playwrights hopes rose, however, when a letter came back posthaste from Mr. Wheeler informing her that the charm of her diction more than atoned for the lack of continuity in the story. It was a good old-fashioned melodrama with the fire brigade featured to a great extent. On the night of the performance in the old Masonic Temple Theater, the amateur playwright received the thrill of her life when she heard her first lines spoken by Virginia Harned and Julia Arthur.

"I remembered how I had thought them out in my own head, sometimes punctuated by the groans of an invalid lodger in the next room, which slightly hampered my inspiration. But they sounded great to me then."

Among Mrs. Shoaff's most cherished trophies are the stained glass windows from the old Temple Theater, which she acquired by a miraculous rescue just as the pickax was about to descend upon them and break them to fragments. For years she had coveted those windows which brought back such pleasant memories. It was sheer luck that she arrived just as the wreckers got to them.

"I went plunging across the street and landed head-on almost in the stomach of a fat good-natured man who seemed to be in charge. Bricks were flying in every direction and some of the windows lay there shattered. At my hurried explanation, my good-natured friend gave some orders and these two windows were saved from the wreckage."

Carrie Shoaff's interest in art had continued so that she was still able to turn out a piece of work with the perfect detail of the old school of painting which dealt with bull-dogs as models to a great extent. She was a pupil of Caroline Woodward and Joseph Dille. She remembered when the Dille studio stood in the middle of an old apple orchard on Home Avenue.

"I recall my first lesson in this old studio, where we paid a dollar and a half for a lesson and could paint all day. I always loved to paint animals, and I got along fine painting dogs, but my first deer looked like a jackass."

Among the artist's most valuable possessions was the oil portrait of George W. Wood, done by Mrs. Woodward, on millboard with its fragile gold leaf frame enclosed in a mahogany shadow-box, now the property of the Allen County-Fort Wayne Historical Museum.

In her studio were also art objects made in Fort Wayne by the old Dreibelbiss Company, an early industry that flourished on Pearl Street in the eighties. The imitation marble composition proved durable as well as beautiful.

All of the causes to which she gave her allegiance had been won by this time. Women's suffrage, prohibition, World War I came so close together as to stun her. She did not belong to the mid-Victorian era in which she found herself.

"I was born too soon, through no fault of my own, and on April 1, at that."

2

In the days when not only the birds of the air but the fowls of the barnyard had nests, and incubators were unknown, Fort Wayne was the happy hunting-ground of many a feathered song-bird. Today it would appear that civilization and the machine-age have made as many changes in bird-life as in the lives of the rest of us.

The passenger pigeons are now only a legend — women no longer wear the remains of birds to adorn their millinery, and the hen's place is no longer on her nest. The incubator has taken over her life-work. All this and more has come to pass in a comparatively short span of time.

Consequently, the story of the migration, housekeeping, nesting and mating of the birds that used to visit the region of our three rivers is rapidly becoming a legend, too. It is the story of the passing and extinction of many beautiful varieties of birds. For civilization has brought its curse as well as its benefits to the birds as well as to mankind.

In 1868, Charles A. Stockbridge began his study of birds in this vicinity. There were great elm, sycamore, and willow trees along the rivers. And within and near the city limits were great groves where the birds came freely each season and made their homes.

Now it is traditional with small boys to take an interest in birds; not always to the advantage of the birds, however. The small boy has won a reputation as something of a savage who needs taming before the world is a safe place for birds and bird nests. Here was a small boy who was different.

Among the books in the library of N. P. Stockbridge, pioneer book dealer of Fort Wayne and father of the bird collector, were a number of books on nature study. So this boy of twelve approached the subject from the standpoint of the student rather than the hunter's or average small boy's viewpoint. He began to *study* about birds.

The Stockbridge bookstore which was a center of culture in its day, was located on Columbia Street along with all of Fort Wayne's early thriving business houses. Nearby was a saloon, the owner of which had an interesting sideline. As chief exhibit in his place of business were several stuffed eagles and other large birds. He was a taxidermist. From him the young bird collector took his first and only lesson in taxidermy. It was just one lesson, but it was a long one. The old man told him everything he knew.

With this as a start, young Stockbridge began the collection. School children who visit the Allen County-Fort Wayne Historical Museum today love to stand in front of the glass cases of birds which form the Stockbridge collection. Most of these first specimens were mounted when Mr. Stockbridge was a boy and at the height of his bird enthusiasm. All of the standards are of black walnut. The later work is mounted on other wood, since black walnut is no longer plentiful.

The private museum was started with specimens of birds reptiles and mammals. Later it was confined to birds and eggs. It became so large that part of it had to be shoved away in the attic of the Stockbridge home where everything from bats to a six-legged lamb was carefully wrapped in paper, standing on its polished wood mounting.

"Would you like to see the lamb?" the naturalist said pleasantly as he began to unfasten the paper wrappings.

"Oh, please don't!" I replied, almost too hastily. Because I am one of the people of this world who has no interest in six-legged lambs.

The collection — first placed in the Fort Wayne Public Library — contained 500 specimens in one large case, which was only a small part of the whole collection. For the collector had identified thousands of birds in this vicinity.

Nothing reflects the progress of civilization more than the changes that have come to bird life. In addition to the fact that shorter hours have been secured for the hen by the coming of the incubator, there have been many other important changes. While the hen has been relieved of certain responsibilities by the machine age, other fowls have not fared so well.

Time was when there was a streak of the savage in the so-called fair sex. Among the principal items of adornment for ladies' hats were wings, feathers, bird breasts and whole birds. Then came progress in the guise of humane propaganda in favor of the birds, and such adornment lost favor. So effective was the teaching that there came a time when women wore no trimming on their hats. An occasional elk's tooth on a good brother's watch-chain was about all that was left of the tendency of human beings in civilized regions to adorn themselves with the remains of birds and animals.

The great loser in the battle against the birds has been the *passenger pigeon*. Even the legends of the flocks that darkened the sky have passed almost out of living memory. The legends are true; yet there has been no authentic report of any passenger pigeons in this vicinity for fifty years, Mr. Stockbridge said.

When he was a boy the passenger pigeons used to pass in the spring and fall. Driven from their roosts in Indiana and Ohio, they took refuge on a stretch of land four miles wide and twenty miles long in Michigan. Here they were doomed. People used to go in boats and stifle them with sulphur. They were fed to the hogs. They were also eaten by their human killers. The most destructive years were 1872 and 1873.

The Mississippi Valley with its fertile land and its great forest trees has always been the home of many bird species. There have been 363 species known to pass through Indiana. In the whole of North America there are 768 species and 400 sub-species.

Among the species that have become extinct are the Carolina parokeet, Eskimo curlew, Labrador duck, ivory-billed woodpecker. The trumpeter swan is almost gone. The golden plover is nearing extinction as are many of the shore birds.

For the birds have followed the frontiers as they moved westward. The bobolink, which was formerly an eastern bird, now is found as far west as Iowa. Like other migrants, including the tourists, the birds always go down the east coast to Florida before coming westward. Most of the Mississippi Valley birds migrate west in this fashion. The western birds go through Mexico in their migrations.

Civilization has brought many changes to the birds. Take the cowbird for instance. The cowbird used to follow the buffaloes across the plains and mountain trails. They would light on the buffaloes' backs and hitch-hike in this way over great distances. Nature, always accommodating, provided the cowbird with an adaptable disposition, something like the modern tourist. As a result the cowbird was willing to move into most any bird's nest. He found moving cheaper than paying rent or owning his own home. The eggs of the cowbird have been found in the nests of eighty varieties of birds.

But with the passage of the buffalo, how about the little winged friend and fellow traveler? The cowbird, adaptable as always, refused to remain unconsolable. He adopted the cow. And he continues to thrive and to keep up his way of life.' The notion that the cuckoo is the only bird that lays its eggs in other birds' nests originated in Europe. The American cuckoo is not that kind of a bird. It is just as well to clear up this little matter.

Most of our birds are native to this country. The only notable exception is the European starling which was imported in 1880 and liberated in Central Park, New York City. Since then they have become very abundant and have extended all over the Eastern United States. Like many immigrants to our shores, they live in cities. They make their homes in buildings and trees and grain. These facts won the attention of the Department of Agriculture. Today all insect-eating birds are protected by law. The crow and European sparrow are not under this protection.

The chimney swift is another bird that has had its habits altered by civilization. Whereas it used to make its home in the decayed trunks of trees, it has had to change its residence because of the scarcity of trees. It now inhabits chimneys and seems to prefer them.

The chimney of the Third Presbyterian Church used to be the residence of a flock of 1,000 of these swifts which Mr. Stockbridge observed at close range for a number of years. They are unable to perch like other birds but cling to a chimney supported on the needlelike barbs of their tails. When the furnace fires were started in October, the swifts would decide to take their flight for a warmer climate. As the years passed their numbers gradually decreased.

It is to the credit of the naturalist that bird-life in America today is protected. A great and rich government cannot afford to be wasteful. The scientist with his proved facts was able to appraise the economic value of our wild birdlife. Birds, at least most birds, were shown to be an economic asset. The insect-eating birds destroyed the insect pests which menaced trees and grain. These facts won the attention of the Department of Agriculture. Today all insect-eating birds are protected by law. The crow and European sparrow are not under this protection.

The law also prohibits the "caging and trapping" of native birds. Foreign birds can be imported for scientific reasons, however. And strange as it may seem, caging wild things does not work such havoc as one might suppose. Animals at least are better off in captivity than in the wild state, Mr. Stockbridge said. That is to say, their life-expectancy is longer. The hazards of civilization are not as destructive of animal life as the hazards of their native wild environment. Civilized man treats them much better than their wild preying neighbors.

It was through the work of Audubon that the idea of humane treatment of wild life was widely propagated. Through the newspapers, schools and the work of all nature lovers, public opinion was won over to the humane theme.

During his lifetime of bird study, Mr. Stockbridge made a collection of hundreds of beautiful specimens of birds, all mounted. Some of the larger birds are a gorgeous peacock, red-tailed hawk, cormorant, starling, immature pheasant, whooping crane now rapidly vanishing, blue heron and many others.

The daily interest of the collector at the time I interviewed him, was in his three large incubators where a total of 36,400 chicks could be hatched at one time. Experiments in new types of brooders, methods of feeding the day-old chicks engaged the attention of the veteran naturalist, whose interest in fowls was still the absorbing passion of his life. For his was the gentle absorbtion of the student who fills his life with an interest that is everlasting.

XIII.
First Woman Druggist

1

It was way back when they used jockey club and patchouli perfumes, and when nice ladies did not use rouge. When a drug store carried mostly drugs and was marked by red and green urns in the window; and sometimes by a gigantic mortar and pestle as distinctive as a barber pole.

The druggists' bill for supplies in those days carried many items that are not to be found there legitimately today. Miss Julia Emanuel has in her possession a wholesale bill of 1871 that belonged to her grandfather, Dr. Jonas Emanuel of Spencerville, Ind. It was found among papers in the original Meyer Brothers Drug Store where Dr. Emanuel used to get his supplies.

At the end of the account which includes cream of tartar, borax, alum, ether, turpentine and all of the items you would expect to find in a drug store, occurs a cheering list. It is as follows: One gallon jug Malaga wine, $2.75; 2 gallon jug cherry brandy, $3.25; 4 gallon rye whiskey, $5.00; 1 gallon alcohol, $2.12; 2 gallons common whiskey at 90 cents per, $1.80.

Such things could be had as a matter of course in the neighborhood drug store.

Miss Emanuel started her drug business in the old Arcade in 1902. Even then all that had changed. And in ten years or more, blear-eyed men used to come into the store with a doctor's prescription and a thinly-disguised story about a sick wife. They didn't want to see her suffer. It was terrible. Couldn't the druggist have a heart and fill the prescription just once more?

But prohibition has not made the only change. New standards of health, beauty and hygiene, have made just as radical changes in the drug business. Things are quite different in these lip-stick days. In the gay nineties when Miss Emanuel worked in Meyer's drug store, only theatrical people used makeup. And they did it at their own risk. Painted ladies were not in good repute either on or off the stage. Women's business in life was not to be beautiful. There was enough of a hang-over from a puritanical age to make that clear.

Soap and a wash-rag were about the only aids to beauty. Apologies were made for the bit of powder one dusted over a shiny nose. The cult of feminine beauty had not yet been developed. Beauties, it was believed, were born and not made. Handsome is as handsome does, was a favorite motto.

The novel idea that it is a woman's duty to be as beautiful as art and nature could make her had not come into wide acceptance as yet. The combination of a good wife, mother, and housekeeper, who had decorative value also was practically unheard-of. It remained for the Twentieth Century to develop a new type. And right here the cosmetician came into his own.

Miss Emanuel was graduated from the University of Michigan in a class of 40 boys in 1889. Her ambition was to be a druggist. She had inherited this ambition from her mother. Her father was a village doctor in Antwerp, Ohio. The country doctor always had a goodly supply of drugs. After her father's death, her mother carried on the drug part of the business. Capsules and pill-boxes, therefor, had been her toys and playthings since she was a small child. She had grown up on drugs, you might say.

During the nineties Miss Emanuel was employed in Meyer Brothers Drug Store in Fort Wayne as the first woman in the retail drug department. The firm occupied an L-shaped building at the corner of Calhoun and Columbia Streets. A saloon occupied the corner location.

In those days the druggist was kept fairly busy making his own pharmaceuticals. Today he purchases these already prepared from the big drug companies. He can put his time in to better advantages in other ways, he finds. The public always has had to have its drugs. It was the task of the druggist to keep the inner man well-drugged and, therefor, healthy. The external man and woman was not of so much importance.

The curative effect of looking one's best had not been recognized generally. When it was, the result was quite important. It not only revolutionized woman's routine, it improved her appearance and possibly prolonged her life. It also gave a new impetus to the drug business and the beauty parlor. It made ugliness a sin and beauty a virtue, thus reversing the order of a previous age.

The drug business profited by the new concept of feminine beauty. The lipstick days came into being. For in spite of all that has been said about drug-store complexions, the fact remains that modern woman manages very well with them, or a reasonable facsimile. It has been established that they are not merely a substitute for a natural healthy skin, they are an aid to it.

It may be that some women have gone giddy over it all.. But don't blame them too much. They may be just getting even with a world that had convinced their mothers and grandmothers that all is vanity, and that vanity is a lure of the devil.

Most of the changes in the drug business, which has had to keep pace with modern living, have come about since Miss Emanuel started. The mere fact that a woman should be attracted to the business is a sign of the times. The emphasis placed on cosmetics was and is an outgrowth of the new cult of feminine beauty.

Yes, the drug business certainly changed after the turn of the century, Miss Emanuel emphasized. Before that women did not spend money on such luxuries as a modern drugstore is able to provide. A dollar an ounce was about as much as they were willing to pay for a good perfume. Now perfumes come from $5 to $20 an ounce. And more!

There were the English crown lavendar, crab apple blossoms and white rose perfumes — favorites of the early 1900's. They were gentle odors that bring back memories of mornings in church as ladies settled their black silk dresses in the pews. All very innocent and refined. Nothing heavy and intoxicating. Personality in perfume was devised by the clever advertiser much later.

Today, every art is employed to produce exotic, subtle, distinctive scents. Slender bottles containing milady's personal perfume are worth a king's ransom. Ponce de Leon's fountain of youth is to be found in small vials and jars in the same drug-store that used to exhibit walls lined with huge bottles of epsom salts and quinine.

Instead of being a sanctuary for the suffering, a place to go for relief from aches and pains, it has achieved something of

Miss Julia Emanuel, the only woman in her class, was graduated with 40 boys in pharmacy from the University of Michigan at Ann Arbor, worked in Meyer Brothers Drug store. This picture was taken at the Barrows studio, July 5, 1893.

the mystery of a magician's palace in a neater and more compact form. One says certain words and departs with a new outlook on life, and $25 worth of perfume in a tiny glass vial.

Modern wizardry has been employed to conjure soaps, bath powders, rouge, all to match milady's hair, eyes, color and personality. High pressure salesmanship and mass production have invaded the boudoir and made luxurious toiletries a necessity.

American womanhood is being glorified not only by the theatrical producer, but by the advertiser and manufacturer of all the aids to beauty. The pleasure, comfort and littlest wish of the modern woman is the goal of an ingenious army of those who are constantly devising new ways of tempting her with novelties. The result of these campaigns, in which the drug store offers the ammunition, is "the skin you love to touch," no more "dishpan hands," ever-alluring eye shadow, in short, the chance to live happily in beauty ever after, and bathe always in loveliness.

With all the catering to feminine beauty aids, that does not mean that the good old remedies are not to be had by those who want them. Nor does it indicate that the nice precision of the skilled prescription clerk has been impaired. But it does mean that a new hope has dawned, and that humankind puts some of their faith in preventing ills as well as curing them. New ways have been devised to push back the hand of time, to avert the ravages of strenuous living. And the chemist, working through the modern drug-store, is showering these blessings of health and beauty everywhere.

There is still ipecac for those who want ipecac, and quinine for those who want quinine. There is also a new glamor for those who find that glamor is a symbol of eternal youth. And those who seek it with all their hearts shall very likely find it in the modern drug store.

It is significant that Miss Emanuel, whose appearance today belies her age by thirty years, still uses her own creams and lotions.

2

"Wonderful character, Charlie was. Loved out-of-doors, loved nature, and how he loved to hunt! We've known each other for 70 years. Chums all that time."

As William Buckles, veteran sign painter, looked down from a window in the Randall Hotel commanding a full view of Fort Wayne's first business thoroughfare, the memories kept crowding. His old friend, Charlie Freese, had just passed away. He couldn't help thinking. And it helped to talk.

"Charlie must have loved this block. He never left it for long. Stayed around here for almost 70 years. He built that building there — third from the end on Columbia Street," as he nodded toward the southeast corner of Columbia and Harrison.

"   "And I think we lived through a wonderful age — from

the canal days to the railroad era, from the time of artificial gas to electricity. We grew up with the town. And Charlie was the kind who loved to hunt. His work as a druggist was very confining, so his only recreation was to hunt locally — liked quail — hunted for the love of the sport. Like a fellow fishing until he has so many he has to hunt up neighbors to give 'em to."

You see in those days everybody had a gun. There was plenty of game then. There's no hunting now — to speak of. There were always two or three gunsmiths around here. And the fellows used to hold trap shoots. Now they shoot at clay pigeons.

"I saw the last load of wheat sent on the canal to Toledo from Taylor warehouse. And I recollect the old-style grain elevator run by horse-power. Boys in those days used to take a sack and make a raid on the pigeons roosting there at night and sell them to the gun club for trap-shooting. And do you know those pigeons finally got so educated that when the trap was spring, they just flew down and walked around. They learned that the ones that flew got shot. So then the trap shooters wouldn't buy them any more."

Mr. Buckles came to Fort Wayne from Bluffton in 1870 when his father kept the Hanna boarding house at the corner of Washington and Barr streets. The house was afterwards used as Hope hospital. Then his father opened the Robinson house, predecessor of the Randall, where he is living today.

"In the same room occupied by Mr. Robinson, the proprietor in those days. Robinson must have been a tanner. For when we took the hotel we found the basement filled with vats used for tanning leather. Oak bark was used in tanning. And the country was filled with oak bark."

The post office and the United States Express both had offices in the building, originally four stories high, of the type you see all along the canal — with sloping roof front and back.

"See those old buildings on the north side of Columbia street different from the rest? They are the only buildings left on that block the same as they were in the seventies. Hill and Orbison's old sign is up in the top floor of that building there, or it was not long ago. Bash's are still in the yellow brick. Remember the sign, 'I'm Ward's Dog. Whose Dog Are You?'

It used to stand in front of the third."

I had to admit I did.

A lot of history has taken place in that old block, both sides of it. The American House, pioneer hostelry, stood where the Wayne hotel stands today. The first bank of the State of Indiana was housed in the basement. The Knights of Zoroaster (a swank firemen's lodge) used to hold their weird initiations in one building with a chute leading down into the canal.

"You can tell the old buildings by their window caps of cast-iron. I've often wondered how they hauled the Joliet limestone used on the buildings across from the Court House on Calhoun Street. Wonderful stone! Strong as flint!"

It was the sign-painter speaking now — 47 years at his trade. He could take a photographer to every building in Fort Wayne and tell him just when it was put up and what stood there before. You've seen the name Buckles on the bottom of many a sign. He started in business with Brimmer, his brother-in-law, in the days when a man learned his trade from a fellow who knew his trade.

"They didn't have schools for such things. Charlie Freese learned to be a pharmacist from a pioneer chemist, Charlie German, who went to the top with a big Chicago wholesale house. After Charlie formed the Dreier Drug Company, there on the corner of Columbia and Calhoun, he never got very far away from this block — except for a day or two hunting."

As we sat and talked, I knew it didn't take second sight for a man to recollect the old days when buses used to run to Hicksville and Goshen and stop at the old Exchange on West Main Street where a movie house stood later. The bus was a slightly modern version of the old western stage coach, with a mailbox on the back, bumpy springs under the two seats, one on each side. Here the passengers slipped and rocked from side to side in a very chummy fashion.

In 1870 there was still a canal boat left for picnics out to the Link farm four miles west, where Washington Road is today. A man by the name of Veight had a real canal boat along in 1872 and '74 which he kept painted white for picinics and the young folks danced on the upper deck.

Nor does it take an archeologist to dig down to the old town lying just beneath the surface of memory where Frenchtown, between Lafayette and Hanna, and Irishtown were "on the other side of the track." These rival groups had their own hand engines and would go to a fire and invariably get into a fight. When they went to the White Fruit House fire they stopped to take a drink, then they stopped to fight, while the fire went right on.

Only a wriggling small boy would know about the log sewer discovered underneath the old canal when Harrison street was put through.

"We were boys together — the last of a circle. Charlie was born here."

And I knew that he had given me a picture that only a sign painter could paint.

XIV.
Fort Wayne's Underworld

The shout, "Stop thief!" or "They went Thataway!" would have done no good in catching a pickpocket at the Pennsylvania Railway station right after the Civil War. For Fort Wayne's underworld hideout — a den of iniquity equipped with trap-doors and secret rooms known as Carey's saloon — was located conveniently half a block north of the depot. It was here the crooks from near and far came and found sanctuary.

If a purse was grabbed from the slit pocket inside a lady's long skirt, or a wallet jerked from a man's vest pocket by a quick hand darting over the victim's shoulder, the direction taken by the running feet was toward Carey's saloon, headquarters of a gang of thirty as skillful three-card monte men, pickpockets, thieves, and confidence men as were to be found at large in this country.

This cesspool of early Fort Wayne was a symptom of post-bellum prosperity in a midwestern frontier town midway in its transition from war to peace. It was part of the aftermath of the Civil War when reckless adventurers on the skirmish line who had mastered poker, casino, chuck-a-luck while sitting in on a game by torch-light, were still as reckless as ever.

Times were flush and money was plentiful. As an important railroad point, Fort Wayne became a natural rendezvous for slickers from New York, Chicago, Detroit, Cincinnati, St. Louis, Indianapolis, Cleveland, and Canada. Gamblers were attracted from every direction. Some of the largest games in the United States operated here.

"Those were indeed lively times in Indiana," wrote Mace Long in his book, "The Converted Gambler," in 1883.

The goings-on in and about Carey's saloon constituted a crime wave master-minded by Ed Ryan, an underworld leader who was notorious as the king of confidence men, and was said to have been tried for murder eleven times and acquitted. Captain Carey, proprietor of the saloon, had enlisted in Canada in 1862 and had been mustered out in 1865, before setting himself up in business in Fort Wayne. In this den, after a drink or so, a trapdoor opened and a blow on the head sent the victim to the cellar to be robbed. Many a sucker was drugged and robbed of his last penny in this dive. A greenhorn carrying a satchel and talking freely about buying a farm proved a likely victim.

During the years 1865 to 1867 when Ryan and his gang carried on with a high hand in Fort Wayne, it was clear that local politics was affected by these crooks who were feared by the politicians. The lavish expenditure of their ill-gotten gains seemed an unmixed blessing to the merchants and businessmen as well, who naturally stood to profit from their patronage. Moreover, the thieves could always get a lawyer to defend them.

While the gang operated on trains of the Pennsylvania, Fort Wayne and Chicago Railroad between Valparaiso and Lima, Ohio, and the Wabash between Fort Wayne and Peru, Indiana, thousands of dollars were squandered freely in local gambling resorts. One of the most famous in the country was the Lodge saloon, kept by John Sterling, a thorough gambler, warm-hearted and ready to help the needy or "skin a sucker" and William Grunauer, a cool-headed player and a man of wide reputation in the gambling fraternity. Their faro game was kept going full blast and frequently ran up to the thousands.

Among the patrons of the keno rooms of Tim McCarthy, noted billiard champion of Indiana, were many of Fort Wayne's most prominent business men. In this game the amateur had no chance to win, so here they were fleeced of their last cent.

Ed Ryan's gang was thoroughly organized by their leader who was described as tall, blonde, and terrific with the ladies. His operators were capable of every kind of trick "to raise the wind," from picking pockets — which was elementary — to the most cleverly-contrived and skillfully-executed confidence games.

The fall of 1865 netted these operators an especially rich harvest. The State Fair, attended by 20,000 people, was held in Fort Wayne that year. Many of these visitors fell into the hands of the cunning thieves and were robbed. When a train arrived, several would jump into the car and begin picking pockets. As fast as they had finished with a man, they would chalk a cross on his coat, so that the "boys" would waste no time on him. He was picked clean.

The accomplices would then "skin the leathers" — that is,

take the money from the wallets — and throw the empty purses on the roof of a shed at the rear of the robbers' saloon. So successful were they, that at the end of Fair week, these pocketbooks when gathered and buried by the "understrapper" or accomplice were found to fill a bushel basket. Upon examination, the fellow found $60 overlooked by the crooks, who were not even interested in such small change. It had been for them more than just a "Fair" week.

Now Ed Ryan, according to the converted gambler, claimed a monopoly in his line. But as in every paradise, the serpent eventually raised its ugly head. Ryan's paradise was no exception. Rival crooks began to muscle in. At one time, the gang leader was considerably put out by the arrival of Dennis Marks, notorious confidence man and city slicker from Chicago.

Marks came with a flock of cronies to share in the spoils Ryan claimed as his own. Ryan resorted to a common trick to drive his rival vulture from the field. The scarecrow he set up was an accomplice known to the initiated as Hoosier Brown.

One winter afternoon, the rival gangster was taken for a ride in a sleigh. The pair drove toward the county asylum — or poor farm — and on their way they met with a battered old customer carrying a caved-in satchel. An artful old hayseed, chin whiskers and all!

"Here comes a good bloke!" whispered the Chicago sharpee. "Let's tackle him!"

They stopped the sleigh and accosted the pedestrian.

"Hallo stranger, where d'ye come from?"

"Wall, I cum from down yonder where I jes sold my farm, 'n I kinda thought I'd go north of town a few miles and buy me another one, since I got the cash money right here in this here satchel to pay fer it."

So convincing was the act that Marks' eyes glistened as the fellow tapped his satchel. Since making up to strangers on the road was a good old Hoosier custom, the farmer was invited to jump into the cutter and ride to town. The three went to a saloon and the drinks were passed. Then Marks attempted to swindle the greenhorn with the old-fashioned lock game. He bet the stranger $1,300 that the fellow couldn't open the lock he had just closed with the assistance of Ed Ryan.

The supposed greenhorn, after some hesitation, took the bet, and placed his money in the hands of Hugh Doty, the bartender. The intended victim readily opened the lock, grabbed the $2,600 and started for the door.

"Stop that bloke, he's got my sugar," shouted Marks.

Whereupon Hoosier Brown drew a Navy revolver, pointed it at the head of the Chicago thief and said with appropriate gestures, "That money's mine. I won it and I propose to keep it."

It was thus that the native Hoosier sharpers found themselves in sole possession of the Fort Wayne area. It was not long, however, until public sentiment was aroused. For one thing, the railroads passing through Fort Wayne experienced a heavy falling off in passenger travel. Detectives were employed but they did no good. The gang had been too much for the big Chicago crooks; how could small town detectives hope to cope with it?

Well, the answer to that question is to be found in the following story from the Fort Wayne Gazette for Feb. 19, 1867; for if the politicians were indifferent to the criminals, the press was not:

"The most exciting event of the winter, at least in the line of accident or adventure, occurred this morning at the depot. The parties to the affair were Mr. Tucker, a citizen of Whitley County, and Ed Ryan, the notorious blackleg of this city. Mr. Tucker was in the city on business collecting money.

"He went to the depot this morning to take the early train for Columbia City and while going into his car, was stopped by some fellows of the baser sort who told him the car he was about to enter was a ladies' car, and he could not go in. They crowded round him and in the confusion Ryan(so says Mr. Tucker) put his hand over his (Tucker's) shoulder from behind, and quickly jerked from his vest pocket his pocketbook.

"Mr. Tucker instantly turned, caught Ryan and demanded his money. But the latter broke away and ran for Carey's saloon north of the depot. Tucker followed in hot pursuit, firing at him twice with a revolver, once as they passed the office of the express company, and again as Ryan neared the door of the saloon, the shot passing through the window and within two inches of Ryan's head.

"In the saloon, Ryan had a few seconds' rest, during which,

as reported by a boy subsequently arrested, he took out the money and burned the pocketbook. Meanwhile, Tucker passed around to the corner or rear of the saloon, and when Ryan, chased by policemen and citizens came out of the back door, took after him again, firing twice as before, one shot cutting a hole through his clothes and the other taking effect in the neck.

"Ryan fell and while getting up or attempting to do so, his pursurer gained on him and took another deadly aim, but failed to shoot as the weapon misfired. By this time policemen interferred so that further shooting was impossible. The ball from the last shot lodged in the neck, checked in its force some by a large button.

"Ryan was immediately brought down to the lockup, accompanied by Mr. Tucker. The ball was extracted from his neck by Drs. Meyers and Thacker. The excitement at the depot was intense, a strong disposition being manifested to lynch Ryan on the spot. The blackleg evidently waked up the wrong passenger this time.

"Mr. Tucker is a plainly dressed man of about fifty-five, a prominint citizen and once sheriff of Whitley County. He is neither a coward nor a greenhorn. Ryan will be tried tomorrow before a Justice of Peace. We understand he offers to compromise the case by the payment of $600. The stolen pocketbook contained about $400. We have no room today for comment."

The rest of the story gathered between 6 o'clock that night and the morning after, was continued in the next week's issue of the Gazette.

"Between four and five hundred workmen from the Pennsylvania shops gathered in force. First they went to Carey's saloon, posted a notice ordering Haynes, the bartender, to move out his family and furniture before night as the building was not likely to stand until morning. Haynes was arrested and lodged in jail as an accomplice, the family was removed to a safer place and somehow, just how, nobody knew, the building took fire. Two steamers and a hand engine and a hook and ladder truck went up to be ready for emergencies. None occurred, however, and the building was allowed to burn down amid the cheers of the populace.

"The wind was high, but no other building was endangered.

Nor were any thieves about that vicinity that evening. It was said that the rest of the gang were warned by a 'committee.' At any rate, they were as scarce as blackbirds in January. It was as safe as a kirkyard," the account continued, and further stated that "they certainly caught a tartar in Mr. Tucker of Whitley County."

The situation had given the citizens an opportunity to take the law into their own hands. However, the vigilance committee was to meet at the court house that night to see that its powers were rightly used.

Even so, it was a good thing for Ryan that his cell was well guarded.

The trial of Ryan before a justice of the peace was so well attended that the benches broke under the weight of the spectators. Pale and haggard, Ryan spoke in his own defense. Had he ever harmed a citizen of Fort Wayne? Had he not given freely to charitable enterprises, supported widows and orphans? Groans and hisses from the crowd greeted his speech.

Then the defendant continued in a more practical vein. Besides, he said, the reported theft of $300 was too small to cause such a fuss.

No less than 400 spectators witnessed the final scenes when the verdict — Guilty! — was received with hearty cheers. Ryan took it rather badly, they say. Bail of $5,000 was provided for his accomplices. But when the next day dawned, Ryan's cell was empty. He had flown the coop, leaving behind a trail of broken hearts.

"Strange as it may seem most of the young ladies in town were in love with him," according to the Charles M. Comparet Memoirs.

It has been said that a bold and enterprising farmer had a lot to do with the finale. Armed with a gallon of coaloil, and an armful of willow switches, he rushed in where even the sheriff feared to tread. Too many of his neighbors had been lured to the robbers' den on their way home from market, and been parted from their entire savings. With switches gathered from a creek, Shawnee Run, that used to run through the south part of town, he had entered the den, laid on stoutly till he had the ruffians on the run. Following the battle royal, he splashed the place with coaloil and set it afire. The gang was thus completely routed and the hideout reduced to ashes.

By Aug. 6, 1867, a local paper reported that "the fugitive is heartily sick of his residence in Canada; he is tired of waiting and watching and wants to go home so badly that, rather than remain an exile in the Queen's Dominions, he declared that 'if convinced the authorities at Fort Wayne would not give him more than two years penitentiary service, he would come over and give himself up'."

An Aug. 31, the Toledo Blade stated — "Wednesday night last the notorious Ed Ryan was arrested in Windsor, Canada, on a telegram from Fort Wayne charging that on Feb. 19, 1867, he in company with three others robbed a man named Alanson Tucker in that city, of $410 in notes and bills. On being taken before a police magistrate, the necessary witnesses from Fort Wayne not being present, the defendant was remanded to jail for six days and the examination will be held as witnesses arrive . . . "

The account continues to relate that while Ryan "was being conducted down to the jail at Sandwich by a constable when the party, having reached a cornfield a little this side of their destination, Ryan leaped from the carriage, plunged through the corn and disappeared. Up to last night he had not been arrested . . . "

After several arrests and escapes, Ryan was brought to Fort Wayne, granted a change of venue and was tried in Wabash. He served but two years of his 14 years' sentence and died some years later in a tavern brawl.

Without their leader, all members of the gang dispersed and came to various bad ends. Without the gang, the gamblers found themselves short of victims; for while thieves robbed the greenhorns, they lost their booty at the gambling table.

However, the indications were that Ryan's gang had not lost their cunning, but had transferred their varied talents to greener fields. The Fort Wayne Gazette for Dec. 12, 1867, while Ryan was out of circulation, reported an incident that had all the earmarks of his disciples' handiwork, this time in Chicago.

"Pickpockets At Railway Depots — Besides the hordes of confidence men who swarm at our railway depots on the arrival of trains from the country, members of the light-fingered gentry can be found who ply their nefarious business with more or less success. No sooner do the passengers alight from the cars than a rush is made by the pickpockets into the midst of the crowd and, while apparently in search of a friend or hurriedly making inquiries, are in reality sounding the depths and contents of people's pockets.

"Passengers should invariably avoid these busy-looking gentlemen and give them a wide berth. A few evenings ago, Conductor J. P. Ames arrived with his train at the Pittsburgh and Fort Wayne depot in Chicago. The passengers stepped to the platform and in an instant some half-dozen well-dressed young men who had been awaiting the train's advent, 'mixed-up' with them and elbowed their way here and there, creating great confusion.

"Ames spotted them at once as pickpockets, and made a jump for the one nearest him, whom he saw thrust his hand into a lady's pocketbook. The thief struggled desperately, and in the encounter cut the conductor's hand very severely with a ring on which was affixed a small sharp blade, an instrument used by professional pickpockets to slit dresses, coats, etc., so as to gain access to pockets. Ames was so badly injured that he was compelled to let the fellow escape."

In spite of the warning, conditions at railway depots continued to get no better. It seems they never learn!

XV.
E. A. Barnes — Expert Artisan

Edward Alexander Barnes was born June 13, 1865, in Dhurmsala, Northwest province Punjab, now Pakistan, formerly British India.

"You see, although I was born on the thirteenth, I have had no quarrel with Lady Luck," he readily admits.

He was just born lucky. But was it all luck? Let us see.

Eddie Barnes was born with a caul, a phenomenon believed by many "to bring good luck and be an infallible preservative against drowning." Among those who cherished the superstition was his Irish nurse who called it a "Lookie cap."

So it would seem he was born lucky.

Although he has been an American citizen since he reached his majority, E. A. Barnes nevertheless must be classified as a cosmopolite. His father was Edward Robert Bigsby Barnes, British Major, and his mother Georgiana Hunter Carnegy Barnes. Major Barnes was a Welshman, born in Capetown, South Africa, who had met Miss Carnegy of Stirlingshire, Scotland, as a guest in the home of her brother, Patrick Carnegy, British government commissioner in the province of Oudh, India.

Without inspecting the family tree which dates back to an Emperor of Constantinople in 1048, we find that London, Canada, Chicago during the World's Columbian Exposition, furnish the background for the pioneering career of the young man who came to the old Jenney Electric Light and Power Company, Brockville, Ont., Canada, April 1, 1889, as "expert artisan," and to the Fort Wayne Works in 1893 when he was twenty-eight.

In fact at no point in the earliest London experience of young Barnes did the word "apprentice" apply. "Articled improver", receiving no pay but a chance to get into dynamo and motor business, was the term. It was also the beginning for this Edison pioneer whose career in his chosen field was destined to stretch out from more than forty years before his retirement.

Edward A. Barnes

And what a retirement!

That story is told by a bronze plaque bearing these words: In recognition of Civil Service rendered the City of Fort Wayne by E. A. Barnes as President of the Fort Wayne Community Chest during the last ten years — 1941.

It was back in the old London days in 1883 when Barnes began to feel that the Edison-Gower-Bell-Telephone Companies of London, where an uncle had given him his first job, offered too restricted a sphere of the electrical vista to a young man of eighteen. The necessary step-up came with the Patterson and Cooper electrical engineers where he received more practical schooling, he is convinced, than at the Polytechnic Institute,

Strand, London, the only place to get the rudiments of electrical engineering in 1882.

Suddenly, he recalls, a world of opportunity exploded in the electrical field generally and his life specifically. In Brighton, England, in 1883, he helped install the scenic railway for Magnus Volks, German pioneer in electric transportation. Next he helped install the Ferranti A. C. System of lighting the underground railway of London, under the direction of "Goulard and Gibbs," engineers-in-charge. When it turned out that the three converters — Mansion House, Aldersgate and Ludgate stations — could not be kept well-balanced, he assisted with changing the wiring from series over to what was then called "multiple arc," a method ahead of the times.

About this time "Iolanthe," an opera by Gilbert and Sullivan, was playing at the Gaiety Theatre, Strand, London. In this production the fairies had on their wings very small electric lamps, fed by storage batteries made by hand — the hand of young Barnes — by winding 3" x 2" x 1" lead plates with flannel strips. The theatre was illuminated on the outside, he recalls, by Paul Jablochkoff candles, 10 inches long, consisting of 3/16" rods of carbon separated by chalk cement. These lights burned like candles, ran about three hours, but were easily replaced.

"Probably the first installations of their kind in the world," he says.

To continue with the pioneering "firsts," Mr. Barnes has written: "I installed in Kingston, N. Y., in 1889, two of the first 600-light 'Slattery' dynamos built at the Kerr Murray foundry, as the Broadway plant had been destroyed by fire. In 1892-1893 I was sent to the World's Columbian Exposition in Chicago to install and run the two operating exhibits the company had there in Machinery Hall, and in the Electricity Building."

In recognition of his skill in installing 500 or more arc lamps on the Midway and 100 in the Electrical Building at the World's Columbian Exposition, a framed diploma hangs on the wall of his study.

"The Columbian Exposition — by an act of Congress — Diploma of Honorable Mention of the United States of America confers — upon E. A. BARNES a certificate having been filed with said Board stating that by HIS skill as AN EXPERT ARTISAN he assisted in the production and perfection of the exhibit of Fort Wayne Electric Co., Indiana which was awarded a Medal and Diploma at the World's Columbian Exposition — 28th day of April, 1894. DIRECTOR GENERAL OF THE COLUMBIAN EXPOSITION."

In the Electrical Journal, Chicago, February 15, 1896, this comment appeared: "It is said that he can make a piece of metal or mica go further than any man in the business; and we all know what economy in construction amounts to."

A lot had happened to Edward A. Barnes to bring about these pioneering firsts in America. When in 1885 the London papers were full of ads of Florida land, Edward, now nineteen, lured by the enticing offers, came to New York and embarked by steamer to Jacksonville, Florida, where he and a companion — an invalid cousin — invested in land and an orange grove. When the year did not prove as fruitful as he had anticipated, he returned to New York with the intention of returning home. On his way to buy a ticket with his mother's check in his pocket, he was startled to hear an American voice saying, "For the love of God, Nevvy!" He stopped in his tracks upon hearing the jesting nickname (British for nephew) by which he was known in his Uncle's telephone outfit in Iondon. He was facing four Americans — all important enterprising young men engaged in building American-made telephones, of which there were only a few in London at the time. They had worked for his uncle with him. He found himself surrounded.

"They seemed tickled to death to see me. It was fate — not an accident — to channel me into a spot where I'd be something — grow with the country."

He was persuaded to stay and take a job with Bergman and Company, New York, then manufacturing supplies for the Edison Company, and furnishing laboratory space in the top floor of the factory for Thomas A. Edison, whom young Barnes had already met in London.

Out of this association with the Wizard came the honored status of "Edison Pioneer," as organized February 11, 1918, while Mr. Edison was living. The objects of the Association as stated in the original draft were "to bring together for social and intellectual intercourse the men who were associated with

Thomas A. Edison in the days prior to and including the year 1885 in his work of invention and experimentation in the arts and sciences; to revive and perpetuate the memories of those pioneer days; to pay tribute to Mr. Edison's transcendant genius and achievements and to acknowledge the affection and esteem in which we hold him."

"There aren't very many of us left," Mr. Barnes adds. "Not more than seven or eight."

In addition to a distinguished father, son of a jurist in Radnor, Wales, who emigrated to Capetown, South Africa, in the early 1800's, Mr. Barnes had an equally notable mother. Georgiana Hunter Carnegy Barnes' family line, according to Debrett's peerage has been traced back to an Emperor of Constantinople in 1048. Edward was about fourteen when he saw his father last, at the time when he had been ordered back to assume the post of District Commissioner of the Transvaal, on account of his knowledge of African-Dutch dialects. His death of diabetes occurred in Kimberly, South Africa, June 11, 1880, when he was forty-six. From England Mrs. Barnes directed the kind of memorial she wanted for her husband. From this time on she devoted her life to her sons' careers. Her younger son, Arthur Allison Stewart Barnes, followed the family pattern, raised a regiment in China, and fought in the Boxer Rebellion.

All the memories of the far-off land of their childhood had come from her lips. There were the other officers' children they had played with; dark-skinned ayahs — so faithful to their young charges; Dadds, their own Irish nurse; and the punkah wallas sitting in front of the barracks pulling the fan ropes with their big toes. When Edward was four and Arthur two, their father was transferred back to England, and they made the long journey by sea from the border between India and Afaghanistan to Southhampton, England by way of Suez and Port Said on the Mediterranean. From then on Kipling's India was pretty well forgotten by the Barnes children who lived in brigade depots at Sheffield Barracks in the north of England, Portsmouth, Bradford, Dublin, Spike Island, Cork, and the Channel Islands off the coast of France. On the River Tay in Scotland where he used to visit his mother's people, he would go with the fishermen to catch herring and codfish. No wonder Edward loved the sea!

And so, undaunted by her responsibilities and eight years a widow, Georgiana E. H. C. Barnes came to the United States in 1888 to be with her elder son and live in Brooklyn, Evanston, Ill., and eventually Fort Wayne. It was her concern and interest that helped to hold him steadfast on his course.

Although he is proudest of his title as Edison pioneer, there are some interesting details of his family line not to be overlooked. For instance, among the branches of his mother's family tree we find the name of Charles Brandon, Duke of Suffolk, and Mary Tudor, Queen Dowager of France and sister of Henry VIII. The Carnegy line descends from Eleanor, daughter of this ill-fated pair.

A collection of ivory miniatures, priceless possessions of Georgiana Carnegy Barnes, includes four generations of the family which has held in entail their estate in Scotland for over 400 years. Ethie Castle, where Edward used to visit with his mother as a child, is even equipped with a ghost that has been known to make the rotogravure sections every time some rash young earl has his name linked romantically with a glamorous title hunter.

As to the natural query, "And what does that make you?", Mr. Barnes' answer begins with a "pooh" and ends "nothing at all." It might mean that his daughters would belong to the upper crust over there, he is forced to admit.

Nevertheless, it is also to be expected that the average American who is the least bit history-minded will be intrigued by certain facts. Of his father's family, they were army men as far back as 1815 when Major General Sir Edward Barnes, adjutant general, and great grandfather of Mr. Barnes, was wounded at Waterloo. His name is among those distinguished guests at the historic Ball at Brussels given on June 15, 1815, by the Duke and Duchess of Richmond on the eve of Waterloo. Remember the lines of Byron in Childe Harold's Pilgrimage?

> "There was a sound of revelry by night,
> And Belgium's capitol had gathered then
> Her beauty and her Chivalry
> And bright lamps shone on fair women
>   and brave men;"

As he sits among his memories and the symbols of a rewarding life, every unpronounceable name of every place and every person connected with his career comes back to him. He is not name-dropping when the names of Edison, Gouraud — Edison's European representative — "Little Menlo" — his residence — Joe, Martin and Samuel Insull occur in his narration. Like R. T. McDonald, general manager of the old Fort Wayne Jenney Electric Light Works, J. J. Wood, its great engineer, Fred S. Hunting, and all the other Fort Wayne associates, they are a part of his life, too.

Should any detail escape him, there are the hundreds of mementoes, photographs and letters. Of these, the leather bound book containing the signatures of his "pals" — every employe of the General Electric Company — is the most prized.

Letters, talks by friends, dignitaries, signatures of individuals and heads of departments, furnish a refreshing reminder of a forty-year career that is unique. The names alone cover many pages of General Electric History. They are: Walter Goll, Manager; J. H. Evans, Perry A. Shober, Fred G. Duryee, Herbert G. Siebold, A. F. Vinson (Squares Club); Departments — Quarter Century, G.E. Volunteer Fire Department organized by E. A. B. 1895, Elex Club, General Electric Band, Foreman's Association, Apprentice Alumni Association, G.E.A.A.A., General Electric Club 1930-1931, Decatur Works— with an embossed page identifying each department followed by the names of the members.

In heartfelt words, Marcus J. Harrigan, President of the G.E. Foreman's Club refers to the "creative thought," "yielding credit to others" as attributes of Mr. Barnes' leadership. "The utmost honor which we may show him is entirely insufficient," he adds. It is his "sincere wish that the Giver of all things good will be kind to Mr. Barnes, so that he may enjoy good health and happiness for a good number of years to come."

Memorable tributes are given also by C. H. Matson, a Certificate of Service from Gerald Swope on the occasion of Barnes' birthday, John W. Eggeman, H. F. Braun, C. M. Niezer, E. A. Wagner, G. E. Emmons, Pasadena, E. J. Graham, Schenectady, H. J. Francis, Walter Evans, Dr. H. O. Bruggeman, H. W. Garton, Helen Stahl, J. H. Heller, Joseph C. Grosjean, T. J. Ryan, N. J. Darling, F. S. Hunting, O. C. Brudi, Esther Moll, Wes Puckett. Marie Blough and Irene Meyers made the presentation of the book.

Then there are the photographs and portraits. A color portrait of Georgiana Carnegy as a young girl dressed in a bonnet and wrap, shows her with all her dreams in her eyes as yet unrealized. There is the Major, his father, as a correct young officer. There is the lad, Bobby, his brother Arthur's son, brought from China at eighteen months on a pillow by the consular British representative on the island of Amoy, off the China coast. Bobby's mother had died, so his aunt, wife of the consul, brought him to Mrs. Barnes to be nursed back to life and health. He stayed with the Barnes in Fort Wayne until he was ten, before he went back to England to his mother's people. Mr. Barnes hears from Bobby from time to time. He went through Dunquerque, the Battle of Britain and all that, as a bombardier in the heavy anti-aircraft battery of the Royal Artillery. His outfit was stationed at Sedan, famed as the breakthrough spot of World War I.

Another story is that of the two daughters, grandchildren and great grandchildren whose pictures accounts of their lives and travels are lively interludes to their grandparents.

The beautiful Mrs. Barnes was Katherine Steinbrunner, 20, secretary to J. J. Woods at the General Electric Company, in 1895, when Eddie Barnes met her and they were married.

As an instance of Eddie Barnes' standing among employees, there is the case of the Bowser strike of thirty years ago.

"The Bowser strike lasted nine years. It took only a few weeks to settle, after doctors, lawyers, preachers, government representatives and other busybodies tried in vain to settle it."

On February 4, 1926, the Business Agent of Mechanists of Friendship Lodge No. 70 took the first step by writing Barnes a letter which included the following statement: "Believing as we do, that you are the one man, who as an employer, understands our aims and policies better than any other employer in our city and that you give us credit for trying to cooperate and of believing in true cooperation between Employer and Employee . . . we are asking you to use your good offices for a try at it at least."

In an exchange of letters, the cause of the misunderstanding was shown to be a statement to be signed by all employees when they went into the company: "I hereby enter the employ of S. F. Bowser & Co., Inc., as above stated and accept the Bowser Plan of Shop Control by Joint Representation."

On March 4, Mr. Barnes requested that orders be issued without delay "to withdraw from circulation these particular cards to which they objected."

On March 8, S. B. Bechtol, President of S. F. Bowser Company replied: "We are ordering a supply of Employment card Record cards, eliminating the objectionable pledge, printed at once so they will be ready to put into use not later than the first of next week."

In less than five weeks the matter had thus been resolved to the satisfaction of all parties concerned.

The jewel in his crown, Eddie Barnes admits, is the G.E. Club House for the workers: twelve bowling alleys, a full gymnasium for basketball, movie equipment (two lamps with automatic shift).

This from a man who says he is too British to be a good mixer, but cherishes the fact that he is known as "the patron saint of industrial amateur athletics in Fort Wayne!"

Nobody but Eddie Barnes can complete his story. So here it is in his own words:

"I always have been for the horny-handed son of toil, the private in the ranks, the worker at the bench, who until quite recently have been the forgotten men in every sense of the word. About forty years ago it was recognized by a few of us on the management side that our greatest asset could be the aforesaid "horny-handed son of toil,' who can always be counted on to give at least as good as he receives, and sometimes even better.'"

"He was a most unusual gentleman and fine industrialist with a particular ken in the field of employee relations," commented Don A. Weber, president of The Deister Concentrator Company, Inc., at the time of E. A. Barnes death August 25, 1959, after serving on the board of that company for 41 years, and after 1926 as Vice-President.

XVI.
First Editions

1

From July 6, 1833, to May, 1863, only three out of seventeen newspapers published in Fort Wayne in 30 years had survived. In a period of untrammelled journalism, fourteen had started out to elect candidates; foster shades of opinion — Independent, Abolition, promote agriculture, literature, Free Masonry, the German language, and had died young.

This is how it all began.

When in January, 1833, the citizens of Fort Wayne felt the need of a newspaper, they agreed among themselves to set the project on foot by securing the services of Thomas Tigar and Samuel V. B. Noel of Indianapolis as printers and editors. Accordingly, Henry Rudisill drew up in his own hand the following agreement:

"We the undersigned agree to become surety for the amount of 500 dollars to be applied to the purchase of a press, to be established in this place and no other purpose whatsoever and we, the undersigned to hold the press, if the said Tigar and Noel should fail to pay it within the year. January 18, 1833. (Signed) — Henry Rudisill, security for 50 dollars, Francis Comparet, security for 50 dollars, A. Hamilton, W. G. and G. W. Ewing, L. G. Thompson, Joseph Holman, John Spencer."

Eight citizens had pledged themselves to purchase a printing-press, when Mr. Tigar acting on his own, bought the press and material on which the Indiana State Journal had been published by Douglas and McGuire prior to November, 1831, at Indianapolis. This paper was of dimensions a fraction of an inch less than the later daily paper, — 21 by 28 inches, to which size it had been enlarged, so that a larger press, chases, rules, etc. were required. So the obsolete equipment bought by Tigar, was hauled from Indianapolis to Fort Wayne through the wilderness. Sometime in the spring of that year, under the editorial and proprietary control of Thomas Tigar and S. V. B. Noel, Fort Wayne's first newspaper was started — The Fort Wayne

Sentinel, with the first issue on July 6th, 1833. The earliest files of this pioneer press are no longer in existence.

The Sentinel — a Democratic paper — was published irregularly until 1837, when G. W. Wood — later Fort Wayne's first mayor, purchased it and made it a Whig paper. This it continued to be until the spring of 1840 when it was sold to I. D. G. Nelson who changed it back to a Democratic organ. After a year or so it was sold back to Tigar.

In the summer of 1840 Mr. Wood purchased another office and established the Fort Wayne Times — a Whig paper — which he continued to run until the fall of 1842 when it passed into the hands of Henry W. Jones and continued to the end of 1844. In March of 1844, Mr. Wood began a campaign paper called the People's Press which continued throughout the presidential campaign, when it was merged in the Times and was called the Fort Wayne Times and the People's Press.

Under several owners this latter paper continued until it became the Fort Wayne Daily Times in 1854 and ran until July 16, 1856. The last owner, John W. Dawson, suspended publication until February 1, 1859, when he started a daily known as the Fort Wayne Daily Times. So far we have dealt with only two papers — the Sentinel and the Times.

But there is more to come. O yes indeed!

There was the True Democrat, started by R. C. F. Rayhouser in 1852, which ran for a few months. The Plow Boy, an agricultural paper, died at the age of two. The Democrat became the Laurel Wreath, a literary paper, edited by Thomas Clark, and sold in 1854 to D. W. Burroughs. The Standard, a weekly paper of abolition politics, and the daily Standard were started in November, 1856 by Mr. Burroughs, who sold out in March 1956 to R. D. Turner. It now became the Fort Wayne Jeffersonian which lasted until March, 1858.

In the winter of 1855 and 56 another literary paper called the Summit City Journal began under the patronage of the Young Men's Literary association of Fort Wayne, and lasted about three months. In July, 1856, a campaign paper, the Fort Wayne Journal, was started by Hood and Kimball, who continued to run it until the campaign ended. In May the weekly Republican was begun by Peter P. Bailey who started a daily Republican in January, 1859. Two German papers — the Fort Wayne

Democrat in 1856 and the Indiana Staats Zeitung in 1856 were published in Fort Wayne. An Evening Transcript lasted about a month in 1858. The Indiana Free Mason, a monthly, printed by R. C. F. Rayhouser and edited by Sol D. Bayless was started in January, 1859.

However, trying times were in store for free and untrammelled journalism. In 1860 Allen County had cast 3,224 votes for Douglas and 2,552 for Lincoln.

Of the 17 newspapers started since July 6, 1833, only three had survived — The Sentinel, a Democratic paper; Dawson's Times, an independent; and the Staats Zeitung, a German paper. A life span of a few months to a few years had been enjoyed by at least fourteen of these victims of journalistic mortality.

The Independent paper called itself "A Whig journal — perfectly independent, with courage to do right and scorning to do wrong."

Obviously, the community was not quite satisfied with the newspaper outlook, for —

In the midst of the Civil War, an overwhelming desire on the part of "certain citizens of this community to maintain a more perfect Union and help Abe Lincoln win the war," led them to a bold venture. They started a newspaper, a Whig paper, the Gazette.

In such a time and for such a purpose, the Gazette was born — in May, 1863 — four pages, six columns to the page.

THE PUBLISHERS WERE D. W. JONES OF GRANT COUNTY, AND ISAAC JENKINSON, PIONEER ATTORNEY. THE GAZETTE WAS HOUSED IN AN OFFICE AT 125 COLUMBIA STREET, "NEXT DOOR TO HILL AND ORBISON 2d. FLOOR," ITS MASTHEAD STATED, AND WAS THE FIRST AND ONLY STRONG UNION PAPER IN THE COMMUNITY.

Next to the dedicated purpose of the determined little sheet calling itself "The Fort Wayne Daily Gazette," the quaint format strikes the modern reader. With all the gravity of the times, the Gazette followed the custom of the day with ads on the front and back pages, and the headlines — messages from the President, Sufferings of our Prisoners, in small print — very small print — on the inside.

OUR PREDECESSORS BELIEVED IN ADVERTISING.

THE IMPORTANCE OF ADVERTISING WAS EMPHASIZED IN AN EARLY ISSUE.

"About advertising—you see goods are like gals—they must go when they are in fashion and good-looking — or else a yoke of oxen wouldn't draw them afterward. Advertise — if your horse, pig, colt, sheep, or oxen go astray. Advertise them right off. Merchants think nothing of paying $40 for one sign with nothing but their names on it. Well, what do you think of having 8,000 signs in the newspaper? In it you show your whole establishment to the country."

AN AD FOR SPIRAL HOOP SKIRTS—CORNER BERRY AND CALHOUN STREETS, OPPOSITE AVELINE HOUSE, WAS SAID TO BE FOR THE FIRST ENTERPRISE OF ITS KIND IN OUR CITY. ALSO "FOR THE LADIES." BIRD CAGES, FINE PLATED WARE, TEA AND TABLE SPOONS, KNIVES AND FORKS, MATTS AND WASH TUBS, CLOTHES WRINGERS, FLAT IRONS, DUSTING BRUSHES, BROOMS, CLOTHES LINES, WASHING MACHINES, MOP STICKS, AND IN FINE, *EVERYTHING* EXCEPT DRY GOODS AND GROCERIES. *AT THE HARDWARE STORE OF B. W. OAKLEY.*

But the "ladies" did more than wash, wring, and iron clothes; for a great movement was formed that drew wide support from all loyal Americans. It was called the Ladies National Covenant. National president was Mrs. James Taylor and vice president, Mrs. Stephen A. Douglas.

DOUGLAS ON HIS DEATH IN 1861 HAD BEEN EULOGIZED BY BOTH FRIEND AND POLITICAL FOE AS A GREAT MAN.

The local organization was formed May 11, 1864, in a meeting held at the Berry Street M. E. church. The signers pledged themselves for three years during the war to purchase no imported article of apparel. The signers who formed the committee to select permanent officers were Mrs. Royal W. Taylor, Mrs. Homer C. Hartman, Mrs. Peter P. Bailey, Mrs. Jesse L. Williams, Mrs. George Humphrey, Mrs. Fred Meyers, Miss Eliza Rudisill and Miss Eliza Hamilton. It was a veritable Who's Who of Fort Wayne society.

PERMANENT OFFICERS WERE MRS. HUGH MC CUL-

LOCH, PRESIDENT; MRS. ISAAC JENKINSON, WIFE OF THE GAZETTE'S EDITOR, SECRETARY.

The avowed aim of the movement was to suppress extravagance, refuse to purchase goods of foreign manufacture, especially jewelry, silks and other finery.

"Costly finery," they stated, "of every kind can be dispensed with. It is a grievous impropriety to send our gold abroad to buy them at the expense of national credit. It is a slur upon the men denying themselves all but rations of salt meat and hard-tack, in the field to put down Rebellion, that another set should roll in luxury meanwhile. Let loyal conscientious people take these thoughts into consideration and a remedy will suggest itself."

One small luxury left to the ladies was kid gloves.

All of this important news on the austerity program, as well as such items as letters with the well-known signature "A. Lincoln" were to be found on Page Two.

For example, under the single word RIGHT was the following: "The President recently appointed two widows of soldiers killed in our battles, Postmistresses of the towns in which they lived, and accompanied the appointments with the following sensible suggestions to the Postmaster General:

"Executive Mansion, Washington, July 25, 1863. Hon. Postmaster General, Sir — Yesterday little endorsements of mine went to you in two cases of Postmasterships sought for widows whose husbands have fallen in battles of this war. These cases occurring on the same day, brought me to reflect more attentively than I had before done as to what is fairly due from us here in the dispensing of patronage toward the men, who, by fighting our battles, bear the chief burden of saving our country. My conclusion is, that other claims and qualifications being equal, they have the better right, and this is especially applicable to the disabled soldier and the deceased soldier's family. Your obedient servant. A. Lincoln."

PRACTICALLY BURIED UNDER THE ADS WHICH FILLED THREE COLUMNS ON AN INSIDE PAGE WERE ELECTION RETURNS SUCH AS: "ABRAHAM LINCOLN OF ILLINOIS FOR PRESIDENT; ANDREW JOHNSON OF TENNESSEE FOR VICE-PRESIDENT." ON THURSDAY, JUNE 7, 1865, FOLLOWING THE

BALTIMORE CONVENTION THE EDITOR DE-
CLARED: "ABRAHAM LINCOLN IS OUR CANDIDATE
FOR PRESIDENT, AND ANDREW JOHNSON FOR
VICE PRESIDENT OF THESE UNITED STATES, FROM
THE 4TH OF MARCH NEXT. WITH THEIR NAMES
WE FLING OUR FLAG TO THE BREEZE, AND KEEP-
ING STEP TO THE MUSIC OF THE UNION, MARCH
ON TO VICTORY. SUCH IS THE REJOICING NEWS
THE TELEGRAPH BRINGS. LINCOLN BEING NOM-
INATED BY ACCLAMATION AND JOHNSON ON
THE FIRST BALLOT. FREEMAN OF THE NORTH.
FREEMEN OF THE SOUTH — FUTURE AGES SHALL
LOOK DOWN ON THIS DAY'S WORK AND CALL IT
BLESSED."

Notwithstanding a vigorous program of nationwide economy supported by the "ladies," there were ads for many new-
fangled contraptions. "Waggoners French enamel — for
beautifying the complexion," and other beauty hints.

"Feminine hair, elaborately frizzled and hanging over the
shoulders like the fleece of a cashmere goat is becoming the
rage at Indianapolis, with an occasional zebra variation," was
one fashion note.

On "the dress movement," they had this to say: "We agree
and we hope that our lady readers coincide with us, that Paris
should not rule the world in matters of dress and it behooves
us to examine the power of the forces marshalled under fashion
and frivolity, who are introducing within our walls another
Trojan horse."

The typical war-time entertainment at Colerick's Hall was
designated by a word of seven syllables — the Mammoth Pe-
lopticomorama. It was described as showing "the horrors of
the battlefield — fierce and deadly conflicts, the din of battles
and the crash of war — are represented with lifelike vividness
— Each scene illustrated with a graphic description by Mr. R.
Grand Barnwell, the talented elocutionist, whose thrilling
powers of description has elicited the highest encomiums of the
press and public. Additional attraction of rain, rippling water,
rising of the moon, the fire and smoke of artillery are, we pre-
sume, that which forms the pe-loptico part of it."

On an inside page was the great "malice toward none," second inaugural speech of Lincoln on March 4, 1865. For over two years the Gazette stimulated enlistments, reported the words and messages of the President, followed the local torchlight processions celebrating Sheridan's victory in the Shenandoah valley, Sherman's march from Atlanta to the Atlantic, Lee's surrender at Appomattox, to the stirring April 9th bulletin proclaiming "the war is over," always on inside pages.

"At Fort Sumter, Henry Ward Beecher, William Lloyd Garrison and Theodore Tilton have raised the flag which four years ago was torn down," was the thrilling news.

In the same issue the editor delivered himself of a stirring editorial — "Hog-pens are the greatest nuisance in the city and if hogs are allowed at all they should be allowed to run wild."

The courageous publishers had supported the war in every way, and then, on the fateful April 15, 1865, the column rules throughout the paper were turned upside down. Black mourning! For just six days after the flag — which four years before had been torn down — was raised over the black and shattered pile that had been Fort Sumter, President Lincoln had been shot.

By October 1865 when the Indiana State Fair was held in Fort Wayne, the waxwork figures of Booth and Lincoln were being shown in traveling museums.

The papers reveal that Fort Wayne was progressing after the war. The White Fruit House which stood between Main and Berry Streets — a frame structure 44 by 64 feet and 20 feet high, with two stories and storage facilities, was a matter of some note at the close of the war.

The new omnibus line — called a "street railroad" — from the Hedekin House to Calhoun and thence to the depot every 15 minutes was a feature of great interest. "Just think of it! From Main Street to the depot for only 5 cents. A man will wear away 5 cents worth of shoe leather in going that distance if he walks, besides losing time and strength that are worth double that amount. Most beneficent arrangement! When our citizens are once thoroughly accustomed to it they will make it a paying concern."

To no man did progress between 1812 and 1865 appear more phenomenal than to John Jackson of Elkhart County, to judge from a communication to the paper, dated March 22, 1866:

"In 1812 having been a soldier belonging to the Ohio troops

under Gen. Harrison, who marched to Fort Wayne in September, 1812, we found a small fort of blockhouses and pickets, with one company of soldiers under Captain Rhea, and all the inhabitants of the place including the soldiers probably 200 in number crowded in that place. All the cabins, fences and improvements were burnt to ashes and their horses stolen, their cattle and hogs killed, their mill burnt, no kind of a hut standing, except the fort — the army was encamped within the bounds of the site of Fort Wayne, and now in the short space of 37 years, it has become a city containing a population of upwards of 21,000, amongst the largest cities in the state."

XVII.
Unity and Peace

1

A garden on the south side of Main Street in the first block
west of Calhoun would be a sight to see in any day. To the
child who remembered such a garden, it proved to be a wonder
garden, a story-book garden, with a mystery about it that she
could never quite forget.

The stone wall with a paling on top hid the garden from her
gaze until she reached the gate and could stop and look inside.
The picture framed by the black iron gate never changed, and
never disappointed her. Inside that fence was a brick house,
and stretching beside it was a garden that sloped down until
it became a sunken garden beyond a fountain spraying on the
wide lawn. Beside the fountain sat an old man smoking a long
curved pipe, and wearing an exotic-looking dressing-gown, and
on his head a fez cap. It was a prayer cap, the child was to
learn later.

The old man appeared to be reading or musing, as a gay
parokeet swung in a brass ring at his side. Not until she was
grown up did she learn that there really was story-book romance
in that house and garden.

Her mother and aunt never stopped long enough to let her
go inside even when the old man had waved at her.

"Laura, are you coming?" a voice would call from quite a
distance. Maybe the parokeet would ruffle his feathers. When
the voice called, she had to pull herself away from that picture
and catch up with them. They had some lining or braid to buy
that day and they were always in a hurry to get it done and get
home. She never could understand why grown folks spent
their time doing such uninteresting things.

Who the old man was she never learned. It was enough for
her just to stop and look inside that fence. Her imagination
supplied the rest.

When she had children of her own, she used to tell them
about her secret garden. Then one time her daughter related
the story at a luncheon in Philadelphia, whereupon a gentle-

man sitting across the table from her and listening intently, re-marked, " That old man in the skull cap was my grandfather and the house your mother saw was the Nirdlinger home back in Fort Wayne, Indiana."

The old man was Frederic Nirdlinger. It was Miss Dorothy Detzer of Washington, D.C., now Mrs. Ludwell Denny, who recalled the story her mother, Mrs. A. J. Dezer, had told her. The man who recognized the description of his grandfather was Charles F. Nixon, playwright and author, son of Sam Nird-linger, who had changed his name from Nirdlinger to Nixon as several members of the family had done.

While the Nirdlinger home which stood on the southeast corner of Main and Harrison Street, has long since been de-molished as the town grew, what it stood for is remembered to this day. It was the home of Frederic and Hanna Nirdlinger, prominent early settlers of Fort Wayne. The house was in the style of an English manor house, with a great living-room containing dark rich furnishings.

Frederic Nirdlinger was a merchant associated with A. Op-penheimer in the largest clothing store in Indiana — the Palace of Fashions, at the corner of Columbia and Calhoun. The Nirdlinger family were called aristocrats. Mrs. Detzer, in her delight with romance, had written from memory her account of the Nirdlinger garden among stories about the Old Gardens of Fort Wayne.

"Not until many years afterward did I learn that there was indeed romance in house and garden — romance that began with the famous Chouteau family of St. Louis, and that is a story in itself," she wrote.

Of Pierre Chouteau, the fur-trader of St. Louis, nothing more is said.

Although a note in a Parkman journal for April 25, 1846, had a slightly reminiscent sound that made me wonder even more if there might be such a connection. Old Pierre Chouteau, co-founder of St. Louis, lived 3 miles out of the city when Park-man visited him and noted: "Found his picturesque French house in the middle of the woods — neat Negro houses, with ver-andas, bird cages hung in the porch — chickens chirping about the neat yard."

Even in mid-century, Mr. Nirdlinger was considered extremely modern, and was a member of the city council way back when the Indians were still around. A street named Nirdlinger Avenue for him at one time, was changed later by the city council.

Nirdlinger, according to a biography of a distinguished grandson, George Jean Nathan, had come from Nordlinger, Germany, settled first in Chambersburg, Pennsylvania, and later migrated to Fort Wayne, the frontier settlement, over the old Wayne Trace. His daughter, Ella, married Charles Narer Nathan of Alsace-Lorraine. Their son, George Jean was born in the house which stood formerly on the northwest corner of Berry Street and Broadway where a new wing of St. Joseph's Hospital stands today.

The story is that Ella Nirdlinger attended boarding school and there met a young woman by the name of Ella Quinlan of Cleveland, Ohio. Miss Quinlan later married James O'Neill and their son was Eugene O'Neill, the playwright, who became associated with George Jean Nathan in American dramatic history.

Although Nathan, founder and co-editor with Henry L. Mencken of the AMERICAN MERCURY, critic and author of many books, especially on the theater, is possibly the most famous descendant of the Nirdlingers, he has no further connection with our story after leaving Fort Wayne at the age of eight.

A recent biographer has this to say of Nathan and his forebears: "He came of wealthy and distinguished family. His father, Charles Narer Nathan, owned vineyards in France and one of the largest coffee plantations in Brazil. Of George Jean's father we know that he married Ella Nirdlinger also of Indiana, that he was a classic example of the wanderlust; that he was one of the finest fencers of his day; that he loved the theatre; and that he was educated at Heidelberg University in Germany. From his mother he must have inherited his inimitable charm and culture."

There are legends clustered around the figure of Frederic Nirdlinger. But even some of them have been lost. That he was quite a wit, Theodore Frank recalled. Mr. Frank's grandmother, Mrs. Meyer Eppstein, was a sister of Frederic Nirdlinger.

"Let's see, how many children have you, Mr. Nirdlinger?" his friends would ask.

"Well Sir, I can't tell till it rains," he would answer slyly.

It was a real pioneer family. There was Albert, an outstanding member of the community; Sam Nixon, the great theatrical man of Philadelphia; Charles Frederic, successful playwright, who graduated from Harvard; Frank, manager of the Broad Street Theatre, Philadelphia; Mrs. Ella Nathan; Eli; Mrs. Dolly Leopold; Max, a member of the Fort Wayne School board for a number of years. Max was founder of the clothing firm of Sam, Pete (Morgenthaler) and Max.

All traces of the home and members of the family have been gone for years except as the Nirdlinger name appears on deeds, and records.

Among the first of the families to have a piano brought to Fort Wayne on the canal were the Nirdlingers. In this connection a story is still told among these early families. The family of Gustave Greensfelder lived close by the Nirdlingers as friendly neighbors. One Sunday morning a maid of the Nirdlingers was sent to the Greensfelder house to borrow four eggs. Mr. Greensfelder opened the front door that led into a long hall to the kitchen. When he heard the request, he called out in a loud voice to his wife in the kitchen, "Fanny, the Nirdlingers have a piano but no eggs!"

The phrase became a byword to fit many a situation in time to come.

However, it is the old Nirdlinger home, with which we are concerned most. It is the beautiful Jewish home life and filial love of this home that is remembered best. In this house was held the first Jewish service in Fort Wayne and in Indiana on October 2, 1848. This richly furnished house proved to be a haven and refuge to the first young Jews who came to this community. There were twelve of them. Since there were no Jewish families when the first of them came, there were no girls here for them to marry. So they had to import wives from Germany, and nearby towns.

The first girl to be born to a Jewish family in Fort Wayne was Terese Redelsheiner — Mrs. Leopold Levy — of Indianapolis, a sister of the late Mrs. Benjamin Rothschild.

Frederic Nirdlinger was among these first young Jews to

Frederick Nirdlinger, Sigmund Redelsheimer, Isaac Lauferty, and Abraham Oppenheimer in a friendly game.

come as far west as Fort Wayne when it was a village of less than a thousand inhabitants. For a livelihood, they peddled their wares, carried their packs on their backs, sold Yankee notions or opened small business establishments. They all built permanent homes in this community. By 1849 with a population of 4400, there were 12 Jewish families.

As one of their own historians has stated: they were willing to brave the trials and dangers of those times to come to the land of civil and religious liberty and to attempt to live their lives free from the fetters of old-world political strife and religious prejudice."

While the chill of time shed its patriarchical frost upon these bearded young men eventually, they were venturesome, strong and hopeful when they came. Since they were strangers in an alien land, they banded together to form what finally became the first Jewish congregation in Indiana. In the preamble of the original constitution, they wrote these words (in German):

"We who like so many immigrants from Europe, have come to these fortunate shores in order to find a refuge against European oppression.

"We who have gone away from our native homes, kinsfolk, and everything that was precious and sacred to our youth, realize when any calamity visits us, that we have left all assistance behind, and that we have been deprived of the last comforts of religion.

"We, the undersigned citizens of Indiana, have bound ourselves hereby to stand by each other in every trouble of life, and to pay the last tribute of respect to our members, under the name of the Society, For Visiting The Sick and Burying The Dead."

The signatures to this document were those of Frederic Nirdlinger, Isaac Lauferty, Abraham Oppenheimer, Sigmund Redelsheimer, Gustave Greensfelder, Isaac Wolf, Daniel Guggenheimer, Kaufman Drucker, Frederick Graffe, Isaac Fisher and Lazarus Lauferty.

The date of the signing of this document was October 2, 1848, under the name: *"Verein Fur Krankerbesuche und Todesbestattung."*

The first legal act of the society was the purchase of a burying ground adjoining what is now McCulloch park, for which the sum of $200 was paid. Since there was no building, on Friday night they kindled the Sabbath light of candles in their homes and were faithful to their Sabbath observance.

It was during the period of eight years before the first synagogue was acquired that Mr. Nirdlinger opened his home for the services. The men of the congregation met in the big front parlor and the women in the smaller rear parlor. This was the beginning of Jewish congregational life in Indiana. The next community to organize was Lafayette.

Not only were services conducted for adults, but instruction for children was given on the second floor of a building across the street from the Nirdlinger home. Meyer Eppstein taught Hebrew and German. Mr. Walter taught English classes. As evidence that boys will be boys in any age, one old fellow recalled the youngster who played pranks on the teacher. This mischievous boy put tar on the steps leading up to the school so that the teacher stuck fast when he tried to go to the classroom.

At the rear of the Nirdlinger residence was the carriage house which held the family carriage in which Frederic Nirdlinger toured the streets of Fort Wayne with Stephen A. Douglas on October 11, 1860.

2

No more impressive event ever occurred in the life of the synagogue than the dedication of the first little frame house of worship on September 23, 1859. The building stood on Harrison Street at the rear of the lot at the southwest corner

of Wayne and Harrison Streets. It had been a German Methodist Episcopal church and accommodated three hundred people.

The pulpit was placed at the east end of the edifice after the
fashion of Solomon's Temple, a procedure which the local
paper explained "was absolutely necessary for all churches of
the Hebrews." The building was a small structure but "amply
large enough," the editor stated, "for the congregation of this
place, and reflects great credit upon those who have planned
and carried out the design. The pews are without doors and
evidently meant to be free to every Israelite, however humble
his condition might be."

The pulpit and Ark were gilded, and two candelabra stood
at the sides. Above the Ark were the Ten Commandments cut
in marble. A central chandelier with twelve lights furnished
illumination. Handsome draperies enhanced the simple inter-
ior. The women sat in the gallery apart from the men, but
were equally diligent in their service to the congregation. The
Thirza Society they formed became the Hebrew Benevolent
Society during the Civil War.

The dedication ceremonies starting at 4 o'clock were participated in by both Jew and Christian. They were conducted in
the strictly Orthodox manner. The entire service was in the
Hebrew tongue, except the address delivered in English by the
Reverend Isaac Leeser of the Portuguese congregation of Philadelphia. For the benefit of those not familiar with that language, the complete English version was printed and distributed
among the audience.

The service was conducted in this manner: The Rabbi
knocked three times at the door and said, "Open for me the
gates of righteousness, that I may enter through them to praise
the Lord."

Then Rabbi Joseph Solomon bearing the Torah with its purple
and gilded knobs and bells, accompanied by Rabbi Leeser and
followed by the officers of the congregation, after reading and
responses by the Rabbi and congregation, made seven circuits
around the synagogue, during which procedure the Psalms were
recited.

"This is the gate of the Lord, into which the righteous
shall enter. How goodly are thy tents, O Jacob! Thy
dwelling-place, O Israel! O, how I love the dwelling-

place of Thy house, and the place of residence of Thy glory. Let us enter His gates with thanksgiving, His courts with praise."

For the first time, friends and neighbors of the congregation heard this familiar Psalm spoken in a strange tongue.

The procession now ended before the pulpit, the Ark was opened and the laws deposited therein, and it was closed. Then Rabbi Leeser exhorted the congregation not to set their hearts upon worldly goods and pleasures but to prepare for good works by holy lives, to reap the reward of everlasting happiness. He stated that "the peculiar people were preserved in the earth for the purpose of God's providence — to keep alive the knowledge of the one God!"

Two years later — in 1861 — the name Achduth Vesholom, meaning Unity and Peace, was adopted. The next year the front part of the location, facing Wayne Street, was purchased for $2,000. As the congregation grew, it was found necessary, by the year 1874, to build a new Temple of the Gothic type. The dedication took place on January 7, 1876, with Rabbi Isaac M. Wise as speaker, in the presence of invited guests including city officials.

At this time the congregation of the First Presbyterian Church made a gift of $1,000 in gratitude for the use of their edifice at the time the Presbyterian Church was destroyed by fire, because no rent or money consideration had been accepted.

On the occasion of the fiftieth anniversary of Achduth Vesholom, a history of the congregation was read which concluded with these words:

"Let us seal tonight a bond of covenant between the generations gone and going and the generations here and coming, that Achduth Vesholom may never falter and that our posterity may preserve and guard it to the Glory of God and man."

To the group coming originally from Germany have been added members from Russia, Poland, Rumania, Holland, Norway, Hungary, England, France, Lithuania, Egypt, Spain, Switzerland, Ireland, Portugal, and Austria.

B'nai Jacob Congregation (orthodox) was organized in 1910.

The distressed in many lands reach out in brotherhood to the members of both congregations today.

XVIII.
On Hearing the Call

1

From a motley collection of log buildings clustered about two trails — the Portage Road to the Wabash and the Wayne Trace to Greenville and Fort Washington — the village grew into a town. The first log house to be built outside the fort was William Suttenfield's in 1815, near the southeast corner of Barr and Columbia Streets. It later became a part of Washington Hall, pioneer inn and land office. From this intersection the village grew in all directions.

In 1818, the same year young Samuel Hanna came to Fort Wayne and built his first log cabin on the northwest corner of this intersection, James Barnett arrived, married Miss Nancy Hanna, a sister of Samuel Hanna, and went into partnership with her brother. Barnett built the first brick house in the village on the north side of Columbia Street near the Hanna trading-house. As Schwieter's bakery, the original house stood for many years.

2

It was six years after the First Presbyterian Church was organized with seven members on July 1, 1831, by Rev. James Chute, that the first church edifice — a one-room frame building — was built on East Berry Street near Lafayette. The little group with a few added members had worshipped during those years at various times in a rude board shelter, in halls, rooms, a carpenter shop, and a tavern on Columbia Street.

The carpenter work on their new home was done by Matthew Griggs, who had accompanied Reverend "Father" Ross, a traveling Presbyterian preacher, in a light two-horse wagon from Franklin, Ohio, the winter of 1822, on a trading expedition with hats and dried fruit. The pair had found themselves in the middle of a prairie during a severe snowstorm, and had led their horses to the village of Fort Wayne, where they found shelter under the roof of Samuel Hanna.

Two of the charter members of the little congregation were Ann Wells Turner and Rebecca Wells Hackley, Captain William Wells' half-Indian daughters, who had been educated among their father's people in Lexington, Kentucky.

In Lyons, France, a young Deacon by the name of Julian Benoit met Bishop Gabriel Brute, first Bishop of Vincennes, who could promise only cornbread and bacon in a New World parish to this spoiled child, accustomed to comfort in his native village in the Jura Mountains. It took young Father Benoit 52 days on a sailing vessel from Le Harve, France, to reach New York on June 1, 1836, on his journey to begin his life work of 45 years in the pioneer post, Fort Wayne. He arrived at his destination by canal.

A young German tutor among the Baltic people in Riga, Russia, in 1843, read in a pamphlet an account of the Lutheran missionary movement among the German settlers in the United States. Three years later, in 1846, occurred the establishment of a theological seminary in the little frontier town of Fort Wayne under Rev. William Sihler's direction. Beginning as pioneer pastor of St. Paul's Lutheran Church, he was to see almost forty-two years of service, among German settlers representing every part of Germany — from East Prussia to the Rhine, from Bremen to the Black Forest.

The bulk came from Hanover, but the market-place was said to have been like the tower of Babel with many tongues when the German farmers brought their dairy products, vegetables, berries, fruits and melons.

The settlers along the western rivers, the fishermen, hunters, trappers, laborers, could never rightly say what year they saw a familiar figure for the first time in this region. It was a fall day, they thought about 1830, when his pirogue daubed with mud and tree-moss, and laden with appleseed fresh from the cider presses back east, rounded the bend of the Maumee River and landed at the foot of Main Street.

How could they know it was going to seem important to anybody to recall just when Johnny Appleseed appeared among them? Yet he worked at his calling — gathering and planting trees and seedlings — until March 18, 1845, when along the St. Joseph River north of Fort Wayne, at the cabin of a friend where he had stopped for the night, his westward trail ended. Yet his lifework was to go on and on!

"The wilderness and the solitary place shall be glad for them," from Isaiah XXXV, was the text of Rev. C. Martin of

Ohio, at the organization of the Isaac McCoy mission of ten members at Fort Wayne into a regular church of the Baptist faith on August 3, 1822. However, with the removal of the mission on December 9, 1822, to a site on the St. Joseph's near Niles, Michigan, the organization became only a statistic.

The Maumee mission organized in 1830 by the Methodists also found it difficult to survive. The first church edifice for this congregation was built in 1840 at the northeast corner of Harrison and Berry.

3

On the day when Stephen A. Douglas came to Fort Wayne in 1860 and rode with Frederic Nirdlinger in the family carriage in a parade which required two hours to pass a reviewing stand, Lincoln was burned in effigy in the Court House square.

But the firing on Fort Sumter at daybreak April 12, 1861, thrilled the north with patriotism. On April 15, Mayor Franklin P. Randall called a mass meeting in Hedekin Hall, in which men of all political faiths joined. Allen Hamilton and Jesse L. Williams were members of a committee on resolutions which stated that, "in the present crisis of our national affairs there should be but one party in the state of Indiana and that party should stand pledged before the country to uphold and sustain, by all means in its power, the national administration, enforcing obedience to the laws and preserving public property and vindicating the honor of the flag."

Five days later, the Stars and Stripes were raised at the Wabash Railroad shops where they remained until the close of the war.

On July 4, 1861, Hugh McCulloch — just twenty-eight years after his first Fourth of July speech — was heard again. "Let the storm blow — let traitors rage and despots in Europe 'imagine a vain thing' — Liberty is still with us, a living principle — the Union though assailed, a reality and, bound together and cemented as the states were by the blood of the Revolution, may we hope that they are indissoluble and imperishable."

Again the Declaration of Independence was read, this time by Mayor Franklin P. Randall.

4

In the year 1866, Schuyler Colfax, Vice-President of the United States, advised young Robert Stoddard Robertson —

born April 16, 1839, in North Argyle, N. Y., and recently discharged from the northern army — to start his law career in the flourishing city of Fort Wayne, Indiana. The three years following his arrival — 1867, 1868, 1869, young Colonel Robertson served as city attorney. From then on he was active in Republican politics in the city of his adoption. He served as Lieutenant Governor in 1886.

Col. Robertson wrote in 1889 in Volume II, History of the Maumee Basin, of the Allen County Bar — "There were giants in those days, mentally and by a course of legal training, under a system which compelled men to think and act quickly upon their own ideas, based upon a knowledge of the basic principles of law and equity without the aid of multifarious tools of the profession of the present day. There was (sic) no law libraries then, such as we find in every county seat today, where for almost every question we may now find, 'Thus saith the law.' At that day the bench and bar were strong in pleading, strong in argument, and among them there was a spirit of courtesy, and of all that goes to make what should always go together — the lawyer and the gentleman. This spirit built up a code of ethics for our bar which has rarely been violated; and then only by the pariahs of the profession."

5

By 1894, the first hundred years had slipped along so fast that there was no time to plan a centennial celebration when the idea first struck the leaders. It was not until October 22, 1894, anniversary of the day Major General Anthony Wayne ran the American flag up over his new fort, that a committee of citizens met with the Indiana legislature. As a result of this meeting, Allen County was authorized to appropriate $2,000 for the centennial celebration. To this sum Fort Wayne added $3,000. Perry A. Randall, prominent local attorney, was named general chairman of the event.

"What One Hundred Years Have Brought to Fort Wayne," was the subject of a masterly address given by Col. R. S. Robertson, at the Princess Rink on October 17, 1895, to mark the opening of the centennial on October 15.

"'In Splendor the Grand Centennial Celebration Is Opened This Morning" were the headlines for the day. "The booming of cannons awakened the slumbering residents of Fort Wayne today," the account began. "One hundred guns welcomed the opening of the grand centennial celebration. The bells in the steeples in harmonious accord rang out their sweet tones and sang praises for our birthday anniversary. Many whistles blew their shrill notes doing honor for the occasion, and giving the keynote for the song of progress.

"The centennial celebration was ushered into a happy beginning at 6 o'clock this morning amid the roar of guns, the ringing of bells and the playful cadence of the multifariously toned shop whistles.

"The glow of a beautiful day kissed the city and the rays of the illuminating power danced on the prettily decorated business blocks and public buildings. What a metamorphosis!"

Electric bulbs by thousands shed their effulgent rays, the article stated. Arches decorated in black and yellow, the centennial colors, spanned the streets. At the intersection of Wayne and Calhoun a grand double arch was erected by the general committee. At Columbia and Calhoun a flaming arch of gas pipes was erected by the merchants in that vicinity. A similar arch flambeau spanned Clinton at Columbia.

Mrs. George D. Crane was chairman of the ladies' art loan and exhibition committee and director general of the centennial building which stood on the site occupied for many years by Wolf and Dessauer. The entrance fee was ten cents to see the exhibits of business and industriy and pioneer relics on the first floor, and the extensive ladies' department and fine arts loan exhibit on the second floor. Here rare paintings, tapestry, glass, wedding presents of 1823, three hundred-year-old heirlooms, needlework, cut glass, china, and floral displays formed an exhibit which compared favorably with the World's Columbian Exposition.

Moving spirit in the affair was Perry A. Randall, who gave the response to the address of welcome of Mayor C. B. Oakley at the Princess Rink.

The morning Journal got out a handsome souvenir edition of twenty-eight pages printed on book paper with portraits of Anthony Wayne and Little Turtle. The week's program included bicycle parades of resident and visiting wheelmen, baseball games between Chicago and Cincinnati teams, an old settlers' campfire where the Philharmonics of 1855 sang, a reception for Governor Claude Matthews and staff at the Randall Hotel, and a great sham battle on October 18.

George W. Pixley, chairman of the invitation committee, received a gracious reply from William Wayne, descendant of Anthony Wayne, the city's founder. At a grand finale on Saturday night, October 19, fireworks at White's field represented the Old Fort, General Wayne, The Spirit of '76, George Washington, the American Flag, and Perry A. Randall. For his part in this and numerous other civic endeavors, Mr. Randall achieved the unique distinction of a monument erected by popular subscription in memory of a life of unselfish devotion to his community. This career ended February 1, 1916.

6

The first hundred years had seen the prosperous little canal town grow into a thriving industrial and railroad center. The founders of its homes and business establishments had come directly from Germany, Switzerland, Ireland, Scotland, England, France, Canada, and many sister states in the Union.

However, the inner life of its people, their thoughts, memories, hopes, are not to be found in the headlines, nor the booming of cannons which awakened the slumbering residents on October 14, 1895, on the occasion of the Fort Wayne Centennial. Even what their contemporaries have said about them is not so revealing as what they have said about themselves.

The Nineteenth Century saw Fort Wayne emerge from a frontier town to a city with the dignity to be expected of her one hundred years. Some of her worries were over, worries of immaturity. She could be lighthearted, shoot off fireworks, and do a little bragging, on her one hundredth birthday.

What was directly ahead of her she could not possibly know. There have been those among us who have tried to tell us what was ahead, to interpret the past, to guide us into the future. Theirs are the voices that will help us to find our way over the threshold of the future.

The voice of Dr. Edith Hamilton, Fort Wayne native and classical scholar, is being heard these days from Greece, Rome and her Washington, D.C. and Bar Harbor, Maine, homes. She is urging us to learn the lessons of the past from ancient Greece. "Greece," she reminds us, "rose to a very great height . . . She rose because there was in the Greeks the greatest spirit that moves in humanity, the spirit that sets men free.

"Plato put into words what that spirit is. 'Freedom,' he says, 'is no matter of laws and constitutions; only he is free who realizes the divine order within himself, the true standard by which a man can steer and measure himself'."

She is asking us not to give up the study of how the Greeks and Romans prevailed magnificently in a barbaric world. Her interpretation of the classics today is full of meaning for those of us who have seen an old world swept away. "The first nation in the world to be free sends a ringing call down through the centuries to all who would be free," she tells us.

Theodore Dreiser heard a different call. In his "Hoosier Holiday" he speaks of this "call and longing to be free."

"This is a most peculiar state. Almost invariably on so-called clear days in July and August out here, an indescribable haze over everything leaves the horizons unaccounted for and the distance a sort of a mystery. This, it seems to me is bound to produce in certain minds a kind of unrest . . . which produces strange new interesting things . . . How else can you explain the fact that 'Ben Hur' was written out here at Crawfordsville, under a beech tree, or why the first automobile course after Brooklands, England, was built here at Indianapolis, or why LaSalle, with a company of adventurers should come canoeing down the St. Joseph . . . into this region? . . .

"Yet I am convinced the old call is still here; and when I return I have a feeling that out here on the farms, driving the cows in the morning and evening in the small towns, and hanging around the old watergaps along the creeks, are boys just like we used to be, to whom the most vital thing in life is this call and longing to be free. Not to be free necessarily or at all of these local experiences, but to achieve a working contact with universal things."

This "call' he speaks of has been heard in many voices. It carries a challenge for all who listen.

It also requires the words of many to give us a true picture of their times. They tell us how the challenge has been met.